PERSONAL PRESENCE

Its Effects on
Honesty and Truthfulness

Joseph T. Culliton
University of Windsor

UNIVERSITY
PRESS OF
AMERICA

LANHAM • NEW YORK • LONDON

Copyright © 1985 by

University Press of America,® Inc.

4720 Boston Way
Lanham, MD 20706

3 Henrietta Street
London WC2E 8LU England

Library of Congress Cataloging in Publication
Data

Culliton, Joseph, T.
    Personal Presence

    1. Identification (Religion) 2.
Interpersonal relations. 3. Honesty. 4.
Truthfulness and falsehood.
I. Title.
BV 4509.5.C85   1985   233'.5   85-6218
ISBN 0-8191-4661-7 (alk. paper)
ISBN 0-8191-4662-5 (pbk.: alk. paper)

ACKNOWLEDGEMENTS

We gratefully acknowledge the use of quoted material from the following source:

Excerpts from <u>The Jerusalem Bible</u>, copyright © 1966 by Darton, Longman and Todd, Ltd. and Doubleday and Company, Inc. Reprinted by permission of the publisher.

TABLE OF CONTENTS

PART ONE: UNDERSTANDING THE FUNDAMENTALS

PART TWO: VARIOUS MODES OF PRESENCE

PART THREE: OVERCOMING OBSTACLES TO PRESENCE, HONESTY AND TRUTHFULNESS

PART FOUR: CREATING A FUTURE IN THE PRESENCE OF GOD

PART ONE

UNDERSTANDING THE FUNDAMENTALS

Chapter 1

BASIC CONCEPTS

People are Relational Beings

Numerous voices today proclaim that no one is an island. This appears to be a very bland assertion. Yet how fundamental a statement is it? Are we really aware of the depth of its meaning and the extent of its consequences? There has been a strong tendency in Western thought to conceive of person or personhood as something encapsulated, as if we exist initially as islands, independent of a whole network of relations with each other, and later find or work our way into relations with things and other people. The ideal male image presented to us is often that of the silent man who stands aloof and independent. We have often spoken as if we can get a basic understanding of personhood as something in itself before taking into account a person's relatedness to other people and things. This is as erroneous as thinking we can know Mary or John without knowing how they interact with other people. Many twentieth century philosophers and psychologists have shown us that this approach to understanding what it is to be human is misleading, and their evidence is of prime importance in understanding personal presence.

Descartes' philosophical starting point, "I think, therefore I am," is inadequate, simply because it fails to take sufficient account of our relational nature. It distorts reality, and should be replaced by "I participate, therefore I am."[1] So too, defining creation as God bringing people (or anything else) into existence is also inadequate. Although it implies relations, they appear secondary. The primary emphasis ought to be placed on God's act of bringing us into relationship with himself and the rest of nature. Being brought into existence is necessarily implied in the latter understanding of creation, but the emphasis is placed squarely on the Creator-creature relationship where it belongs, and the tendency to conceive of people and things as existing independently of this relation is overcome.

John Macmurray maintains that the impulse to communicate is an infant's sole way of adapting to the world. Although this impulse is implicit and unconscious, it is sufficient to establish the mother-child relationship as the basic form of human existence. This relationship is a personal mutuality, a 'you and I' with a common life. All a child's later experiences are also fitted within this same framework of personal mutuality, so that human experience, in principle, is shared experience and human life, a common life. Within the structure of human behaviour, there is always a reference to the personal other. Thus, the unit of personal existence is not simply an individual person, but two in personal relation with each other.

There is also a great deal of symbolic activity in the mother-child relationship, which cannot be explained on the basis of either useful or organic needs or purposes. A mother fondles, caresses and plays with her child just for the joy she receives from doing so, and the baby's responses of delight have no biological significance either. It often cries simply to convey its need for its mother's presence. These symbolic actions express the mutual delight of both the mother and child in their relationship, one which they enjoy for its own sake. The relationship which unites them in a common life is an end in itself.2

This same point can be developed in a slightly different way. Neither an individual person as such nor a group as such form the fundamental fact of human existence. Considered by itself, each of these is an abstraction. An individual person is an existing fact in a living relationship with other people. A group is a fact of existence, because it is composed of individuals relating to each other. Thus, the fundamental fact of human existence, and that which characterizes the human world, is people in relationship to or in the presence of each other.3 The findings of numerous psychologists support this position. They indicate that even be-

fore an infant becomes aware of itself as a distinct
individual, it has begun to experience relationships
with other people. In fact, it is only through such
relationships that infants become aware of their own
individuality.

There is never a moment, then, in human existence
when we exist apart from our relations with others.
The self is constituted by and continues to exist in
relationship with others.[4] People are social to
the core. We can neither become ourselves nor know
ourselves apart from our relations with others, and
there can be no reality for us apart from these vital
relationships. How could I live a human life if I
never met other people with whom to interact and
share? It is clear that we cannot even possess human
life apart from relations with others, because reality is living, and living is the mutual giving and
receiving of our being or life through personal encounters. This is achieved most directly through
relations of mutual knowledge and love. Thus, we can
see that the activities of knowing, loving and enjoying each other, simply for the sake of doing so,
are absolutely essential to the process of becoming
fully human. They are ends in themselves and, as
such, are self-justifying.

The most humanizing and direct interactions we
can perform are our acts of mutual knowing, loving
and enjoying each other. These acts in particular
enable us to become authentically human. In the
sense that they help us develop ourselves, they can
be regarded as means to an end. Nevertheless, the
end toward which they are directed is not something
other than themselves. Life is oriented toward
fuller, richer life, that is, toward fuller, richer
communication and community. Our mutual acts of
knowing, loving and enjoying each other are not directed toward producing anything of utilitarian value,
and ultimately this is why they need no justification.

Other actions and relations, which are entered
into for a useful purpose, also have a value in themselves. Nevertheless, their ultimate value and justification ought to be determined in terms of what
they contribute to the enhancement of conditions that
foster the non-utilitarian, personal relations discussed above. We are relational beings. In our deepest, most personal interactions we become most fully
ourselves. It is in this context, therefore, in

which deep, interpersonal relations are acknowledged
to be of primary significance in fostering human
life, a context in which functional relations are
subordinate to personal ones, that we shall conduct
our inquiry into the relationship between personal
presence, honesty and truthfulness. However, before
we search for the meaning of these three basic realities, let us ask ourselves a few fundamental questions about dishonesty and untruthfulness. These
questions will create a context that will help to
orient our search and make it more fruitful.

Dishonesty and Untruthfulness: Problem or Mystery?

The vast majority of North Americans maintain
that honesty and truthfulness are highly valued goods
that must be cultivated if society is to function at
all, let alone to function effectively. We acknowledge a tendency in ourselves toward selfishness and
greed, yet, at the same time, we loudly affirm that
people have a built-in desire for honesty and truth.
We proclaim our belief in the fact that if people are
honest and truthful, others respond to them in like
manner. Yet dishonesty and lack of truthfulness are
widespread in all aspects of our public and private
lives.

Department stores and supermarkets openly acknowledge that they are forced to add at least fif-
teen per cent to their prices in order to cover
losses due to theft. Manufacturing burglar alarms
and devices to detect shoplifting have become multimillion dollar businesses. Large industries lose
millions of dollars annually, because major decisions
are made on the basis of misleading information. The
real facts are concealed from top level administrators not only by labour, but also by lower levels
of management itself. This is so, partially, because
administrators on lower levels cannot get at the
truth themselves and partially because they are
afraid to disclose many facts to their superiors for
fear of unfavourable consequences 'to themselves.
Wherever we go, we are surrounded by guards, plain
clothes detectives, handbag or parcel checkers and
night watchmen. Perjury is not uncommon, even among
top-ranking officials who hold responsible positions. The concept of a credibility gap has arisen
because we feel we cannot place confidence in our

fellow citizens. This gap extends far beyond political and industrial matters; it also permeates
family communications and interactions. In the light
of these facts, are our beliefs and affirmations
about honesty and truth simply further proof of our
dishonesty and our capacity to deceive even ourselves? I think not. Such a judgment is too extreme.

Honesty and truthfulness are not simple realities.
They cannot be understood apart from insight into the
mystery of what it is to be a person. Similarly,
dishonesty and untruthfulness are not simple problems,
nor, in fact, are they simply problems. It seems to
me that our failure to come to grips with the dishonesty and lack of truthfulness in our society is partially due to the fact that we conceive of them primarily, if not almost exclusively, as problems for
which we can arrive at solutions or answers with the
aid of improved legal and technological methods and
devices.

Certainly preventing shoplifting and bank rob-
beries is a problem for which relatively successful
solutions or answers can be developed by the use of
electronic devices. Preventing students from cheating on examinations and their parents from cheating
on their income tax are also problems for which relatively successful ad hoc solutions can be devised.
However, gaining insight into why we cheat, at the
same time as we acknowledge our built-in desire and
need for honesty and truth, is not simply a problem.
Here, we are not looking for a solution or an answer,
but for meaning and increased insight. These can
only be gained by confronting our experience of the
mystery of what it is to be human.

So too, we are forced to confront the mystery
involved in personal interactions and communication
when we try to gain insight into the ways in which
specific social conditions, and even the entire social
milieu, make being honest and truthful increasingly
difficult. Thus, it is inadequate to continue
treating dishonesty and lying simply as problems for
which we can provide solutions. Looking at them apart
from the insights that can be gained from analyzing
them in their broader, human context is merely applying bandaids to serious sores in our society without trying to get below the surface and diagnose their
real causes. We cannot continue indefinitely to multiply lie detector tests, more comprehensive income

tax laws, safety devices, burglar alarms and guards
and supervisors to supervise the supervisors. Has
not the law of diminishing returns been operating in
these procedures for some time already? Are not dishonesty and lack of truthfulness symptoms of something
much deeper and widespread in our society, and is it
not time we seriously explored every avenue that might
shed light on their causes?

The most fundamental thesis of this work is that
honesty and truthfulness are inherently related to
the mystery of personal presence. Without a serious
attempt to understand what it means to say that people
are present to each other and to gain insight into
the various modes and degrees by which personal presence is achieved, we cannot grasp the consequences of
these modes of presence on our behaviour. Without
this knowledge, we can only grasp a very superficial
understanding of what causes us to proclaim that truth
and honesty are highly regarded ethical and social
values at the same time that we lie and cheat with
religious regularity. Sure, people lie and steal to
get that extra dollar. But to say that the causes of
dishonesty and untruthfulness are simply our greed
and immorality is a vast over-simplification. Recognizing our sinfulness is a necessary beginning, but
the motivation behind these actions is far too complex
to allow us to be satisfied with such a facile explanation of their causes.

When we are confronted with a mystery, we start
by gazing upon a few basic truths. As we continue to
reflect on our experience of these, we see their relations and extensions to other truths and to other
areas of experience. We see connections that were
formerly unseen. We start with a few facts that are
given and many unknowns, and our insight increases
and meaning is achieved as the scope of our vision
broadens and deepens. We start to see what the
pieces are and how they relate or fit together, so
that we begin to develop a global picture of reality
that will take a lifetime to complete, and then only
imperfectly. When confronted with a problem, we
begin with many known or given facts, and basically
one or two unknowns, which must be further isolated
and identified, and then studied in their relations
to the knowns. The procedure or process of inquiry
is to relate the knowns in such a way as to solve the
unknown. The answer is obtained by a movement that
successively narrows our focus until we can zero in

on the factor to be analyzed.

Obviously this contrast of the methods involved
in confronting a mystery and a problem is over-
simplified. Yet, hopefully, it will help us to appreciate why it is essential to start with people as
relational beings, and then turn to the mystery of
personal presence--a mystery which is at the root of
all personal communication and sharing--if we are to
study dishonesty and untruthfulness. By our research
into the various modes of presence and their consequences for honest and truthful action, we can gain
insight into the complex, personal relations and
social conditions that lead us to find meaning in
dishonest and untruthful behaviour. These insights
have to be grasped before we can even appreciate the
scope of the problems involved, let alone search for
answers.

This work promises only an initial road map or
guide through the complexities of personal presence
and the numerous consequences that the various modes
of presence have in motivating either honest and
truthful or dishonest and untruthful action. It will
bring to light a number of facts that are the necessary starting points for research into how to correct the dishonesty and lack of truthfulness in our
society and offer some recommendations, but it will
not attempt to provide solutions to these problems.
Keeping people honest and truthful are problems. The
fact that we are more human and society more humanizing when we are honest and truthful flows from the
mysteries involved in personal presence. Let us see
what meaning can be attributed to honesty and truth
when examined in this context.

Honesty

Far too frequently our understanding of honesty
is restricted to the behavioural level alone. Honesty is described as integrity and straightfor-
wardness in thought, speech and conduct, and as a
refusal to lie, steal or deceive in any way. These
definitions are accurate, of course, but an adequate
understanding of honesty cannot start with the integrity of external behaviour. By starting there, we
merely plunge into midstream and miss the source from
which that integrity in conduct flows. Let us get

back to the source of honesty, to its broadest
meaning and foundation. Only after starting there,
can we appreciate its place within the whole mystery
of human life and its intimate connection with personal presence.

In its most basic or radical form being honest is
being oneself. To be honest, one must accept and be
in touch with oneself. That is to say, honesty
starts with an awareness and acceptance of one's own
person, one's own perceptions, feelings and experiences. Only people who are willing to take the
risks and experience the pain involved in being themselves can be honest with themselves and truly present to themselves and to others. Such people alone
can be honest with others, because in relation to
others, honesty is the direct communication of the
actuality of one's own being, the expression of one's
real self. If I am not even present to myself as I
really am, how can I possibly be really present to
anyone else?

Before going further, let me emphasize that
people are always in process. The self emerges; it
is always incomplete and in process of becoming. So
too, the virtue of honesty is never fully formed. It
too must develop along with the self. Thus, at any
stage in my life, honesty involves striving to know
myself as I am at that time, accepting myself in my
incompleteness, and communicating or expressing that
self. Without a sincere effort to be honest in this
sense, reality becomes distorted and personal growth
is deterred. Yet, even in our homes, a not too subtle pressure to hide our limitations and keep our
best foot forward in all circumstances is pretty
common. Are we aware of the price we are paying for
keeping up this facade in terms of eroding self and
mutual acceptance, destroying honesty and hindering
personal growth?

Honesty characterizes us and enables us to create
an authentic identity and to communicate genuine personal presence to each other. It also enables us to
establish authentic, lasting bonds with each other.
These benefits are achieved from day to day through
the stands we take on the issues that confront us,
through acknowledging our own feelings and through
expressing our own ideas, values, beliefs and convictions. The result of continued honesty is awareness of our individuality and personal value. Thus,

when we are honest, we are really vital or alive and
our presence is felt by those whom we encounter.
Without honesty, there is no presence, no flow or
sharing of life and no possibility for growth or new
life. Dishonesty moves us in the direction of becoming shallow and hollow.

Revealing ourselves to others as who and what we
are does not imply revealing everything about ourselves. In fact, it requires a great deal of
practical wisdom and, at times, considerable re-
serve. Nevertheless, it does imply that we exclude
pretense, exaggeration and what is inauthentic from
our communication. Above all, it demands that when
we express ourselves to others we give them a share
in our being. Where authenticity in interpersonal
communication is absent, those involved are not present either to themselves or to each other in an honest, genuine way. Their behaviour is not merely indifferent or of little consequence; on many occasions
it is outrightly destructive.5 There are instances
in life when my sense of what is fitting tells me I
should really make myself present to a particular
person. When I fail to live up to this awareness, I
deprive myself of the growth in generosity, authenticity and other qualities I could have fostered in
myself by acting. I also injure the other person by
denying her/him the acceptance, support or whatever
else s/he needs.

It is evident from what we have said that honesty
is intimately connected with love. In fact, it stems
or flows from love. If we love ourselves, we can be
honest about ourselves, first with ourselves, and
secondly with others. On the other hand, failure to
love ourselves leads to an inability to be truly present to ourselves and creates a deep, pervasive dishonesty at the core of our very existence. A lack of
self-love also causes us to be dishonest and untruthful in our interactions with others.

People who do not love themselves cannot be present to themselves as they really are and be content
with that. They find little satisfaction in themselves. They do not conceive of themselves as lovable and, too frequently, do not experience themselves as loved by God or by other people. The more
they lack the satisfaction that results from union in
love, the more they feel compelled or driven to
achieve a multiplicity of satisfactions to fill this

insatiable void at the heart of their existence.
Thus, their need to make themselves presentable and
lovable forces them to try to cover up what they dislike in themselves. They constantly try to present
themselves, if not to themselves, at least to others,
as something other than who and what they are. This,
in turn, leads to lying, to exaggeration and to deceptions of many kinds. They are not only dishonest
and untruthful in word and deed, but more important
and more regrettable, they are dishonest and
untruthful in their very being and in their mode of
presenting themselves to others. There is no easy
way to put an end to this behaviour.

Those who do not have a healthy love of themselves appear to be greedy. They seem to love themselves too much (not too little), to center everything around their own needs and desires, and finally, to grasp and appropriate everything to themselves. Because they do not receive the self-affirmation, acceptance and gratification they should
receive from deep personal relationships, they experience an exaggerated need to achieve fulfillment
in other ways. As a result, their excessive need to
obtain satisfaction from possessions easily leads
them into dishonesty in personal and economic trans-
actions. Their need to prove themselves and make
themselves lovable makes them overly competitive; and
where competition increases, so does the temptation
toward dishonesty and lying. These people are under
constant pressure. They try to build themselves by
building empires for and around themselves. Nevertheless, since these material accomplishments cannot
fill their emotional needs, this too is an unending
road that leads to more and more duplicity. Much of
the inauthenticity, unhappiness and lack of communication among highly successful professionals and
suburbanites in our midst is illustrative of the lack
of love of self and the resultant behaviours we are
discussing here.

The phrase "credibility gap" was coined to desig-
nate our lack of confidence in government officials
and administrators, because they present themselves
to us as something other than what they are. However
serious that situation may be, the most disastrous of
all credibility gaps exists within each one of us and
among us and our closest friends and loved ones.
These gaps exist because we constantly present ourselves to ourselves and to each other as who and what

we are not. By doing so we reduce the trust and confidence on every level throughout our whole society
at the same time as we multiply the dishonesty within
it.

If we are serious about reducing the dishonesty
in our midst, the first place to start is by increasing our own love and acceptance of ourselves and
each other. Parents and teachers must help children
to accept what and who they are. We must stop prom-
ulgating the false myth that everyone can get to the
top and that that's what makes us real people. Dishonesty and lying cannot be reduced until we no
longer feel driven to be something other than who and
what we are or can reasonably be expected to become.
Nor will they be reduced until we no longer feel compelled to succeed and prove our value and lovableness
by whatever means.

Basic honesty gives us a stable, constructive
image of ourselves, and helps us to be more effective
in coping with the world around us. We have seen on
a deeply personal level why this is so. Those of us
who are at home with, and therefore united with ourselves, are present to ourselves and to others in a
very integral, constructive way. Hence our basic
honesty and our capacity for personal presence are
firmly grounded. The integrity in our very persons
enables us to perform honest acts, and in turn these
acts tend to further consolidate us as persons.
Action not only flows from being; action is truly
conduct. It conducts or moves us to become the type
of people who perform a particular kind of action.
For instance, when we perform honest acts, those very
acts increase our honesty and strengthen, rather than
weaken, our capacity to perform even more difficult
acts of honesty in the future. Thus, our continued
honesty enables us to become more and more integrated
as people and to develop even more positive images of
ourselves. These qualities are absolutely essential
for our continued success.

What we have said about honesty as an acceptance
of our own personalities and an expression of our
real selves to others indicates why the test of our
honesty is being honest with ourselves, not simply
being honest with others, especially when we are
being observed. People who have developed their
moral character and attained a high level of emotional maturity practice honesty on a rational, al-

truistic basis. They try to examine their acts objectively to see if they serve the good of others as well as their own good, before they decide that their acts are honest. Such action is quite different from honest acts motivated by expediency, fear or conformity. A person who chooses to perform an honest act, after thinking of the good of all those involved, is acting freely. The one who performs an honest act out of fear or because someone is looking is coerced, and is acting more like a slave than a free person.

Before moving from honesty to examine the meaning of truth, let me develop my analysis of honesty one step further by extending it very briefly to discuss two points on the specifically religious level. We have already indicated that understanding creation as God bringing us into relationship with himself is more adequate than understanding it simply as God bringing us into existence. We saw the superiority of the former understanding in terms of its immediate focus on the Creator-creature relationship. The Judaeo-Christian tradition teaches that God created all reality and continues to maintain it in existence. We cannot exist apart from a relationship with God. In fact, this tradition teaches that this relationship of dependence on God for our existence is so central to our very being that it is the first and most fundamental of all our relationships. It is central to our self-understanding and identity. We live in dependence on and therefore to some extent in the presence of God, even if we are unaware of it or consciously deny it.

If this Creator-creature relationship is so fundamental to our self-understanding and identity, that is, if we are God's creation before we are anything else, then is not acknowledging this relationship at the very core of our honesty? There is a genuine difference, on the one hand, between the positions of the intellectual atheist and agnostic, who after serious, conscientious, intellectual search have concluded either that there is no God or that they cannot know of God's existence, and on the other, the position of the practical atheist who has reached no conscientious position on the matter, but in practical daily life lives as if God does not exist. Even if I regard the positions of the conscientious, intellectual atheist and agnostic to be objectively erroneous, I acknowledge personal integrity and hon-

esty in their respective stances. Can I say the same
of a person who has slipped into a way of life that
is that of a practical atheist, out of shere indifference and for reasons of practical convenience?
At least it is reasonable to ask if there is not a
widespread, but unconscious and indeliberate dishonesty pervading her/his whole life? So too, if
practical atheism characterizes an entire society, is
it not reasonable to suspect a pervasive, though unconscious and indeliberate, atmosphere of dishonesty
at the base of that society?

In a similar manner, we might also suspect a
degree of dishonesty, even if unconscious and indeliberate, in individuals and in a society that try
to deny the reality of sin in people and in the world
as a whole. We simply cannot deny the cold fact of
our abuse of and inhumanity to each other. Nor can
we deny that greed is at the core of so many of our
problems. Yet, is it adequate to simply attribute
the dishonest behaviour in our society to greed and
sin? In order to be sinful, an evil act must be conscious and deliberate. As we move forward with our
analysis of honesty, truth and personal presence, we
shall see that much of the behaviour that appears to
be motivated by greed is motivated by other causes.
Thus we shall have to return to these theological
questions again later in our inquiry.

Truth

Ordinarily, when we think of truth, we think of
accepting the truth, contemplating it and above all,
telling the truth. The truth is what is right. It
is a concept, word or statement that is conformed to
reality. The other side of the coin, of course, is
that truth also refers to the reality which manifests
itself to our minds as it is. It is a true colour,
desk, proposition or whatever and has revealed itself
as such; therefore, our concept of it is true. This
brief analysis characterizes, in general, the approach to truth that has come to us from the Greeks.
It has played an exceedingly important role in the
development of Western culture. We are deeply indebted to it. However, it is not the only approach
to truth that is part of our tradition.

Although most of us are less aware of the depth

and richness of the approach to truth that is to be found in both the Hebrew and Christian scriptures, it too is an integral and important part of our North American heritage, and something we cannot drop from our view without immeasurable loss. The Greek philosophical and Judaeo-Christian religious approaches come at the topic in different ways, yet they complement one another. I shall concentrate primarily on the concept of truth found in the scriptures, because its close connection with honesty, as understood above, and its significance regarding personal presence and the relational nature of people make it more relevant to our inquiry than the central tenets of the Greek understanding of truth of which we are more aware.

The origin of the biblical concept of truth is not human experience, but the encounter of people with God. Emil Brunner shows that the scripture approaches the whole question of truth from the perspective of encounter. Divine truth has been revealed or come to the human race from outside itself and from outside the universe in a personal, historical event. For the Christian, the entire process of God's self-revelation throughout the Hebrew scriptures has come to its fulfillment in the incarnation of the Word of God in the person of Jesus Christ. Ultimately, this is the foundation and source of the Christian understanding of truth, an understanding that can be perceived only in an act of faith. In revealing and communicating himself in Jesus of Nazareth, God gives himself to us out of love; and in the very same act of encounter calls us to respond. This call to be answerable or responsible reveals the depths of our human nature in that we are transformed into responsible, spiritually free beings. We are called to obedience to Christ as Lord and impelled to constantly transcend ourselves at the same time as we remain sinful, and therefore inclined to remain within our own very limited horizons.

The perception of truth as encounter with God is faith. We not only have the opportunity to know truth, but through the self-communicating love of God can be or live in it. This creates a fellowship between God and us and among ourselves. The false freedom of autonomy and the self which attempts to possess its own truth within itself are seen to be a lie. Truth happens; it is an event that liberates, because it restores us to our true being--being and

life in and for God. If we are firmly established in
the truth, we understand ourselves as persons and
recognize each other as sisters and brothers.6

Moving from this general overview of truth as
encounter, we see that the Hebrew word for truth de-
rives from a verb that has as its fundamental meaning
to be solid, sure, worthy of confidence. We find the
symbol "rock" used to indicate that God in his person
and in his word is truth. "Rock" symbolizes the un-
shakable firmness of God and his word. Thus, truth
is a quality of that on which we can rely, that which
is stable or proven. Yahweh, in contrast to the
pagan gods, is a moral God. The aspect of moral stability associated with truth indicates why truth is
associated with God's covenants, promises and active,
historical relationship with his people.7 We see,
here, as we have already seen with honesty, that neither honesty nor truthfulness are first and foremost
characteristics of action. Most fundamentally they
are qualities of people. God himself is a rock; in
his very being he is firm, moral and truthful. Therefore, truth flows over into and characterizes his
interactions with his people.

When applied to God, we find that truth is also
understood in terms of fidelity. Here it refers to
the fidelity of God who calls us to place our confidence in him. God's word, covenant and oath are
unbreakable, totally reliable; therefore, they are
true. The "truth of God" means that God's infinite
love for his creation manifests itself in action, and
that divine action is sure, forever stable.8 This
aspect of the Hebrew concept of the "truth of God" is
very significant, because it associates love and
truth. God's infinite love is what motivates him to
speak and to act on our behalf. God speaks the truth
in love and out of love, and his action is eternally
reliable. We also see here that the biblical concept
of truth extends beyond a mere telling the truth to
doing or living the truth. God is truth and all his
action is true. We too, as we shall see, are called
to do the truth, to body it forth not just in word,
but in everything we do.

In the biblical sense, the notions of solidity
and stability are always central to the meaning of
truth. Truth means the pillar on which a building
rests, the support a baby receives in its mother's
arms. True peace is an assured peace, and the true

path is the one that leads reliably to one's des-
tination. What is true is what has been tested and
proven reliable. In this sense, truth is not so much
opposed to error as to lying, deceit, vanity and anything that lacks consistency. Truth is a very broad
concept that also designates sincerity, loyalty and
reliability. In the truthful person, there is
nothing of duplicity, insincerity or guile. Thus,
doing the truth extends beyond acknowledging the
truth of things intellectual to include conforming
our conduct to the truth of things. In the biblical
sense, truth must pass from conviction into practice. A word is true if it expresses our thought
accurately and we are true if we keep our word.[9]

At times, truth also refers to the comportment or
bearing of a just person. When attributed to a
person, truth designates someone who is worthy of
confidence, capable of discharging weighty responsibilities. Here again, it is a question of a
very fundamental attitude of fidelity. Truth is associated with justice in this regard, so that the
person who does the truth or walks in truth is one
who faithfully observes the law of God. But this is
not all. In the scripture, doing the truth is not
accomplished by simply being faithful to the covenant
and law alone. To do the truth we must be faithful
to the fundamental order in the universe and in
society. This not only requires fidelity to our relationship with God, but also fidelity to all our relationships with each other.[10]

To understand this dimension of doing or living
the truth, we must look to the close connection in
Hebrew thought between truth and goodness or kindness. Goodness expresses the notion of loyal dedication in personal and social relationships and
interactions. To this dedication the concept of
truth adds its own connotation of stable fidelity.
"Goodness and truth" or "loving kindness and fidelity" always go hand in hand in biblical thought.
They combine; "to do goodness and truth" always involves a fidelity characterized by and expressed in
acts. Only those who do the truth can hear the transforming word of God and believe it. They share in
God's life and holiness; truth in them is a source of
freedom. Thus we see, once again, the intimate connection between being, knowing and doing. "To do
goodness and truth" is a biblical formula which expresses the idea of unwavering attachment both to the

people involved in an activity and to that which is
to be accomplished. It is a formula that expresses
promise and alliance.[11]

Throughout the scripture, we find numerous examples in which that generous, loyal stability which
is truth triumphed over ambition, resentment and
anger. The father, the friend and the patriot do or
live goodness and truth, when, in spite of their an-
imosities, they act in a manner that is faithful to
their paternity, their friendship, and their responsibilities as citizens. The attitude and behaviour
of David toward Absalom, Jonathan and Saul is but one
example of doing truth and goodness.[12]

In Wisdom Literature, truth designates revealed
truth or wisdom. The law itself is truth as is the
plan or will of God. Thus truth is closely associated with mystery, and knowledge of truth becomes the
object of hope. This concept of truth is further
developed in the New Testament. In John's writings,
God is light and Jesus is the light of the world. As
such, he is the revelation of the truth of God. John
emphasizes the vitality and the inner dynamism of
revealed truth.[13]

Once again, in both John and Paul, we find that
truth also refers to moral conduct and is closely
associated with love. John picks up and develops the
ancient biblical expressions "doing the truth" and
"walking in the truth." To do the truth is to be
directed by the truth and to act according to the
precepts of Christ. We love our neighbours in truth
when we love them by virtue of the dynamism of truth
inherent in ourselves. Paul stresses that Christians
cling to the truth in love. We cannot continue to be
faithful to the truth of the gospel without that love
of God and neighbour which bind and commit us to
truth in action. It is the power of the indwelling
Holy Spirit, who proceeds from the truth, that leads
us as believers to act in accord with it. True
action flows from our interior attachment to the
Truth (God) and bears witness to it. Thus, doing the
truth is not a theoretical, but an existential reality based on a commitment of our whole selves to be
authentic and to perform the kind of action required
to foster personal presence with God and our neighbour. Doing the truth is a practical activity that
is impossible of attainment without enlightenment and
conversion.[14]

The goal of truth in word and action is to increase the love among us. God and people only reveal themselves out of love; thus truthful communication has the effect of increasing love within the speaker, in the hearer and in the whole community. Only where word and love are in harmony can intellectual and moral fellowship exist. Communication that does not flow both from love of what is good and from love of neighbour cannot ground fellowship. Doing or living the truth, therefore, is both community-forming and community-sustaining. Paul reminds us to "practice the truth in love," which indicates that expressions of what is factually accurate are only expressions of truth when they are fruitful in love. Truth is turned to evil when we wield it like a club in a heartless, calculating manner that hurts others and damages relationships. The connection between truth and prudence, discretion and silence becomes evident in this biblical context in which truth, love and goodness go hand in hand.[15]

As you have been reading this description of the biblical concept of truth, I am sure you realized that behind it lay an anthropology, a specific understanding of what it is to be a person. You may also have recognized that the basic tenets of the biblical concept of person implied in what has been said about truth are fundamentally the same as those set forth earlier in this work. Neither the philosophical analysis of people as relational beings nor the understanding of honesty set forth earlier are based primarily on either biblical or theological evidence. Nevertheless, they paint a picture of what it is to be human that is identical to that implied by the biblical understanding of truth.

Both the more philosophical reflections and the biblical evidence presented above help us to see how central honesty and truthfulness are to the vast mystery of what it is to be a person. It is simply impossible to grow as a human being or to be authentically present to oneself or others without striving to be honest and truthful. In revealing why this is so, the relational approach to personhood has a distinct advantage over the approach that conceives of the individual-in-isolation as the basic human unit.

If the person-in-isolation were the fundamental human unit in society, we could gain a true knowledge of ourselves by simply being in touch with ourselves

(our own thoughts, feelings, experiences), and by
being truthful in acknowledging these to ourselves.
In other words, we could gain an adequate knowledge
of ourselves apart from what we learn about ourselves
through the feedback we obtain from our encounters
with other people. We have seen, however, that the
basic human unit is not the person-in-isolation, but
the person-in-relation to others, and that we can
only become ourselves and know ourselves in and
through these relations. Thus, the truth about ourselves is learned, not simply by being in touch with
our own inner reality, but at the same time by revealing ourselves truthfully to others and receiving
their responses.

Let me make it very clear that we are not talking
of any form of total self-revelation here. It is not
the quantity, or even the depth, of what is revealed,
but its authenticity, that creates genuine presence
and results in truth. In an interaction with you, if
I present myself in word or action with insincerity,
inconsistency or guile, your impression of me is
false. Nevertheless, it is on the basis of that impression that you must respond to me. Your response,
therefore, misses the mark insofar as it cannot be
directed toward me as I really am. If I continue to
present myself inauthentically, the further the interaction between us progresses, the further we move
from a relationship based on solidity and stability
--the further we move from doing the truth.

So too, if children are not allowed to accept and
face their negative emotions and the unpleasant facts
or truths about themselves, they cannot be in touch
with their own, inner reality. Children who have
been taught to simply repress these feelings, or to
deny or lie about them, are hampered in their growth
in truth and honesty. They are deprived of the opportunity of seeing both the effects of these emotions on others and their responses. In the long run
there is also danger of a loss of self-love and self-
respect. They come to question whether people could
love and respect them if they knew how they really
felt or thought. Thus, stability within their own
being and fidelity and mutuality in their relations
with others are also endangered. To varying degrees,
and in various ways, inauthenticity, dishonesty and a
lack of truthfulness creep into the very fibre of
these children's relationships with others, even when
there is absolutely no conscious or deliberate effort

to deceive.

We must also learn to perceive each other without either filtering out or judging some facets of what is being made present to us. Where rejection and judgment occur in the very process of perception, that is, where there is prejudice, we never see or accept others as they really are. Once again, any personal interaction under these circumstances is necessarily based on a lack of truthfulness. Our failure to perceive objectively and accept others in their unique otherness is one more cause of our constant failure to be really present to each other and to live or do goodness and truth.

People are really relational; the basic human unit is not an I-in-isolation, but an I-in-relation to others. From this most fundamental fact of existence, it necessarily follows that the truth of all our relations has to include at least a minimal element of altruism. If my analysis of a situation is determined on the basis of the good to be achieved for me alone, without consideration of the good of the others involved, my analysis is purely and simply not true. The intimate connection we have already seen between truth and love and truth and justice indicates why this must be so.

In this chapter we have looked at a few basic concepts. We have explored the fundamental notion that a person is a being-in-relation. We have seen that dishonesty and untruthfulness are not simply problems, but realities to be examined in the light of the mystery of what it is to be human. We have also looked at the expanded meaning of honesty and truth when seen in this personalized context, and not merely as acts people perform. Let us turn next to the notion of presence. First, I shall set forth a general concept of presence; and then, within its broad context, examine physical and personal presence.

Notes

1. John V. Taylor, *The Primal Vision* (London: SCM Press Ltd., 1963), p. 50.
2. John Macmurray, *Persons in Relation* (London: Faber and Faber Ltd., 1961), pp. 60-63.
3. Martin Buber, *Between Man and Man*, trans.

by R. G. Smith (New York: Macmillan Co., 1965), pp. 202-03.

4. Macmurray, pp. 17, 24; Helen Oppenheimer, *Incarnation and Immanence* (London: Hodder & Stoughton, 1973), pp. 132, 137-39.

5. Clark E. Moustakas, *Loneliness and Love* (Englewood Cliffs: Prentice-Hall, 1972), pp. 118-19.

6. Emil Brunner, *Truth as Encounter*, second edition (London: SCM Press Ltd., 1964), pp. 18-21.

7. Charles J. Galloway, "Doing the Truth in Charity," *The Bible Today*, No. 38 (November 1968), pp. 2641-43; Jean Giblet, "Aspects of Truth in the New Testament," *Truth and Certainty*, ed. by Edward Schillebeeckx and Bas van Iersel (New York: Herder & Herder, 1973), p. 37.

8. Galloway, p. 2643.

9. Galloway, pp. 2641-42; Giblet, pp. 36-37.

10. Galloway, pp. 2641-44.

11. Galloway, p. 2644; Giblet, p. 38.

12. Galloway, p. 2645.

13. Galloway, pp. 2645-47; Giblet, p. 37.

14. Galloway, pp. 2646, 2648; Giblet, pp. 40-41; Bernhard Häring, "Truth in Conduct (To Do the Truth)," *On Being Responsible: Issues in Personal Ethics*, ed. by James E. Gustafson and James T. Laney (London: SCM Press Ltd., 1969, p. 146.

15. Häring, pp. 149-51.

PART TWO

VARIOUS MODES OF PRESENCE

Chapter 2

PRESENCE

A General Concept of Presence

Since personal presence is a very complex reality, we shall approach it from many angles; but
first we shall begin by setting forth its general or
fundamental meaning. This understanding of presence,
which is basically Whiteheadian in origin, includes
personal presence; but extends far beyond it. It
explains how inanimate and living things are present
to each other and to people.

The world is not composed of a variety of things
each of which exists as a relatively distinct, complete reality with a minimum of relatedness and dependence on other things. In fact, the exact opposite is the case. The universe is one process of
becoming in which all the parts are organically related or linked in some way with one another. Everything is in process, or more specifically, everything
is in process of becoming itself; and everything is
intimately related and deeply dependent on other
things in order to succeed in this adventure. Absolutely nothing in the universe exists or could possibly exist apart from its relations and interactions
with other things.

Things and people, therefore, are events each of
which exists in what we might call its own actual
world. This world, of course, is only a very small
portion of the whole of reality; but it consists of
all those beings, forces, influences and energies
with which a thing or person has in some way inter-
acted in its past and which, therefore, have enabled
it to become what it is in the present moment. Nothing is ever static. Everything is constantly inter-

acting with and experiencing other things. These
processes vary in duration and intensity, but each
culminates in a satisfaction or consummation which
may be either a growth or a diminishment. At any
rate, the very processes of becoming constitute the
reality of each thing throughout its development.[1]
Thus, it is to each thing's interactions and experiences of other realities in its world that we
must look to understand the most fundamental notion
of presence.[2]

One thing is present to, or more accurately, present in another to the extent that it has played or
is playing some role in the other's process of becoming. A thing is present to another in a causal
role, insofar as it is a cause that contributes to
the internal constitution of the other. When we
speak of presence, therefore, we are speaking of an
influence or influx that effects ontological change,
that is, change in the very being of the thing or
person involved. A thing is present to another, when
in some way it enters into or takes hold of the
other's very becoming. Since presence is fundamentally playing a causal role in the constitution of
another thing, there are varying degrees and ways of
being present. These are as numerous as the ways in
which one reality can influence another.

Presence may well imply proximity in time and
space; yet these are not necessary. Forces, energies, things, ideas and people can have a profound
influence on our becoming and yet be separated from
us by vast distances and even by centuries. In spite
of their lack of proximity, they become part of our
actual world. For instance, the thought of the Greek
philosophers and the ideals of Jesus Christ are woven
into the actual world of Western culture and, even
today, are present to individuals, influencing them
one way or another. The values and goals set by
grandparents and parents, as a result of their experiences of two world wars, influence youth today,
in spite of the fact that these wars are foreign to
their experience.

Presence is not a one way street; there is a mutuality involved in it. The manner and degree of
presence in any encounter are subject to the nature
of the realities that are present to each other and
to the existential conditions in which their encounter occurs. Let us illustrate this by discussing

the presence of A to B. To start off, A can only act
upon B, and so enter into it or take hold of its becoming, according to modes of operation that are limited by A's own nature, capacities and dispositions.
Then too, the external circumstances in which B experiences A may be such as to either enhance or diminish not only A's activity, but also B's capacity to
be open to and receive it. Influencing and being
influenced, like giving and receiving, involve mutuality and complexity. A must be capable and dis-
posed to give of itself to B in a manner in which B
is capable of receiving that gift, if an exchange is
to be completed between them. In other words, A must
be open to playing a causal role in B's becoming, and
must present itself to B in a manner that enables B
to take hold of it. If A is not willing to interact
with B in this way, B's process of becoming, its
structure and constitution will be different from
what they would have been. This may or may not be
injurious to B. There is always the danger, however,
that A's lack of openness to B will leave gaps in B's
experience and in its constitution. It may even
cause deformities, wounds and scars that will interfere at later stages of B's career.

We have spoken so far as if the reality doing the
influencing is more active than the one being influenced. That is, we have spoken as if A is more
active than B. Yet this is not perfectly accurate.
To grasp the nature of their encounter correctly, we
must realize that the thing in process of becoming
itself (the thing encountering and being influenced
by other realities) takes a very active role in its
own becoming. B is very active in experiencing not
only A, but also all the other realities in its
world. As it experiences A among a multiplicity of
other things, it actively selects, rejects and determines the specific manner in which it will take hold
of these realities and allow them to become part of
its constitution. It does this in accord with its
own subjective aim, its goals and needs at that particular point in its development. Thus, B may experience A negatively; that is, it may experience it
as having little or no relevance for' its development
at this time. Therefore, it will not allow A to
enter into it in a positive manner. This rejection
does not imply, however, that the encounter is totally devoid of influence on B. The absence of whatever A could have offered B conditions B's process of
development. B's present and future development

would be different if it had allowed A to influence
it more positively. Thus, as indicated earlier,
there are enduring consequences to the way things
allow others to be present to them at any stage in
their lives.

It is evident from what I have said above that
presence involves a very complex process of interiorization. As a thing strives to become itself, it
encounters realities outside itself, and experiences
all their positive and negative qualities. Many of
these appeal to it, and in the process of making
these qualities its own, it transforms and interior-
izes them. They become part of its very interior
structure. This fact reveals the immense power that
things, and especially people, have over each other
for better or for worse. We have the opportunity to
influence or mold the very structure of each other's
personalities by our mutual presence.

Once we understand our presence to other people
in terms of our mutual capacity to take hold of each
other's becoming, we can begin to fathom the extent
and depth of our mutual opportunities, challenges
and responsibilities vis-à-vis each other. This notion that presence is achieved through mutual influence and interiorization is a central theme that
runs throughout this entire book. Now that I have
described the broadest, most fundamental meaning of
presence, a meaning which embraces the influx by
which things as well as people enter into and alter
each other's constitution, we shall turn to the more
restricted area of personal relations by examining
physical presence.

Physical Presence

I shall proceed in my analysis of the concept of
presence by distinguishing between physical and personal presence. We have already seen that there can
be a presence between people and things, because the
latter can and do play a causal role.in our development. This, of course, is a physical, not a personal
presence. In a similar manner, when two people are
in physical proximity to each other without any effort to communicate, they are physically present to
each other. One can hardly say that we are personally present to each other in any real sense, when

we are merely physically juxtaposed or within view of
each other. What could we possibly mean by saying
that those who stand within view, but refuse to get
involved when someone is being robbed or beaten, are
personally present to the victim?

When we have just met or when our attention is
directed toward matters other than communication with
each other, we can say that we are personally present
to each other, but only in a restricted sense. To be
personally present to each other in the fullest
sense, we must have entered into dialogue with each
other. Here I am using the word dialogue in a very
specific manner. In this sense, dialogue is communication directed toward achieving deeper, mutual
self-understanding. When we are personally present
to each other in the fullest sense, therefore, our
attention is directed primarily toward each other and
the communication between us is that of mutual self-
revelation.[3]

We see immediately that the concept of personal
presence is a very complex one. It must be understood in terms of a spectrum. On the extreme closest to mere physical presence, there is a minimal
personal presence between those who have just said
"hello" or acknowledged each other by some word or
gesture. On the opposite extreme, there is a full or
concentrated presence between those who, through word
and action, have or are manifesting themselves to
each other in a dialogue which is a mutual self-
revelation. Between these two foci, there is a great
variety of degrees and ways in which we are present
to each other. Having very briefly situated the various degrees of personal presence along a spectrum,
one end of which is adjacent to physical presence, we
shall focus our attention on the latter. By examing
physical presence first, we can prepare a basis for a
richer understanding of the complexities of personal
presence.

There is a tendency in discussions on presence to
skip over physical presence very quickly after simply
pointing out that we do not refer tó things or to a
person and a thing as being in each other's presence,
when these terms are understood in their full sense.
Such a scanty analysis of physical presence is incomplete and totally inadequate for understanding how
presence is related to truth and honesty. If we
start with the fundamental Whiteheadian notion of

presence as we have set it forth above, we soon see
that we ought not to underestimate the significance
of physical presence in forming the deepest recesses
of our personalities. Things as well as people are
part of our world and act as causes in forming our
inherent personality structures. Let me illustrate
this point.

John Cowburn, in *Love and the Person*, points out
that a person and her/his suitcase are not, properly speaking, together. This is true, but having
said it, we must realize that we have not denied that
the suitcase may well be present in that person in a
very profound way. Our interactions with things are
heavily laden with a great variety of feelings, and
emotional tones are of major importance in the way
our personality structures and images of ourselves
are formed in and through these interactions.

A suitcase is part of almost everyone's experience. Yet the emotions aroused by the sight of
one's suitcase, and the specific interiorized presence that it has in each person at any particular
stage of life, are very different by reason of the
different causal roles suitcases have played in each
person's becoming. The suitcase of the person whose
family had to move frequently or split up, because
they could not pay the rent, immediately makes present all those feelings of insecurity, shame, poverty
and inferiority experienced during youth. These have
become an important part of who that person is. The
sight of her/his suitcase is heavily laden with emotion. It is a very important symbol for her/him,
because suitcases have helped to mold her/his vision
of reality, image of self and personality structure.

For a transient, a suitcase may be the dominant
symbol by which he identifies himself. The mere
sight of his suitcase, or the job of throwing his few
belongings into it, might well make present deep feelings of loneliness and worthlessness. Cowburn is
right; we do not speak of this person and his suitcase as being together. Nevertheless, the suitcase
beside him on the curb is interiorly present in him
in a very personal way, because it symbolizes his
economic insecurity and inability to develop satisfying and lasting, personal relationships. On the
other hand, for another person, a suitcase may symbolize holidays, travel and good times with the family.
A suitcase has contributed toward the structure of

this person's becoming in a very different way. The
emotional response, the attitudes called forth and
the behaviour motivated by the sight of her/his suitcase are much more creative. In this instance too,
the suitcase is simply physically present to the person, but it is present in her/him through what Whitehead has called "causal efficacy" in a very different
way from that of the other two people we have discussed.

These three illustrations demonstrate how a material object, such as a suitcase, can enter into and
influence a person's process of becoming, and therefore be present in that person in a specific way.
They also bring to light a number of other significant points regarding presence. Certainly all objects a person encounters, or even the same object
encountered at different stages of a person's development, do not have the same influence on her/his personality structure or image of self. The manner and
situation in which a thing is perceived influence the
intensity and type of emotions that become an integral part of that perception. Thus, there are
major differences in the way different perceptions
take hold of different people and become present to
them.

Some perceptions play a much more dominant role
in shaping our personality structures and images of
ourselves than others. Since the emotional element
or tone of an experience is of major importance in
determining the effect of an experience on us, emotions are critical elements in determining how objects are present in us. Undoubtedly, the positive
emotional tone associated with a suitcase, for the
person who had used it for travel, would be less intense, and certainly less cutting, than the emotional
tones associated with a suitcase for the other two
people. Thus, we can presume that the traveller's
experience with suitcases, and their presence in her/
him, played a lesser causal role in her/his psychic
constitution. "Suitcase" would not be a dominant
symbol or one that is central to that person's perception of self and the world.[4]

Beyond the range of our relations with things
lies another whole realm of interactions with people
that is also restricted to mere physical presence.
In order that presence exceed the physical and enter
the personal realm, we must manifest an openness to

each other. One person must take the initiative by
offering a gesture or word indicating a willingness
to reveal her/himself (at least superficially) to the
other, and the latter must respond in a similar
manner. Where this mutual openness is not present,
there is a nothingness, a void or absence on the personal level. This is not to say, however, that such
encounters have no effect on those involved.

In many situations, communication is not normally
expected, so that its absence does not leave any detrimental consequences on those involved. Nevertheless, in far too many instances, the void, the cold
impersonality which confronts us like an icy surface,
is an inadequate and depersonalizing substitute for
the personal presence and communication that should
be there. Physical presence alone, in situations
where there is a need for communication, has profound
negative consequences on us. To understand why this
is so, we need only recall that the basic human unit
is a person-in-relation to another, not a person-in-
isolation.

All of us need to relate successfully with
others. We need to be known and accepted in a deep,
personal way. Yet anyone who has lived in the coun-
try or in small towns has firsthand experience of how
smothering a situation can be in which everyone knows
everyone else's personal life and business. Many of
us literally fled to large urban centres, because we
needed space to be ourselves and to pursue our own
choice of lifestyle with the freedom that urban living affords. City folk, and especially we apartment
dwellers, frequently avoid personal relationships
with our neighbours as a matter of principle. We
almost need what might well be described as the best
of two worlds simply to survive. The world of freedom, privacy and autonomy is preserved by maintaining
as low a profile and as high a degree of anonymity in
relation to our neighbours as is possible. Some of
us conceive the ideal in this regard to be nothing
more than physical presence or proximity. Our other
world of deep, personal relationships and intimacy is
restricted to our families and to the personal
friends we choose. More frequently than not, they
live at a healthy, breathing distance from our front
door.

Beyond the anonymity and autonomy desired by most
city dwellers, our society places a great deal of

value on efficiency and mobility. By and large, we
pursue these with earnest regularity. Yet their widespread achievement is accompanied by, or more accurately, accomplished by, a progressive impersonaliza-
tion of both our social and economic interactions.
The effect of all of this, as the sociologists know
far better than I, has been the progressive spread of
impersonality to more and more facets of our lives.
This has occurred at a time when young people are
frequently cut off by great distances from their families, when pressures on married couples in particular are increasing rapidly and when satisfying
personal relations both within and outside marriage
and family life are being eroded.

None of us can be friendly or open to everyone we
meet, even on a very superficial level. A high
degree of impersonality is inevitable and necessary
in urban living. If we are going to live in big
cities, we have to face the fact that we are necessarily limited to maintaining a physical presence
alone in relation to hundreds of people with whom we
rub shoulders daily. Yet we still have to ask
whether the almost complete autonomy we cherish so
dearly is an unmixed blessing. Can we continue to
pursue it without reservation? Is it possible to
maintain a neighbourhood today that is not at least
to some degree also a community in which people
relate with each other personally?

Increased inflation, unemployment, crime and the
excessive competition we face in every facet of our
lives today are just a few of the factors that create
an excessive amount of pressure, insecurity and
anxiety. Whether they are speaking of life on the
street, economic or even professional life, we hear
people speak of "life out there" as dominated by "the
law of the jungle," "the survival of the fittest."
Such expressions should make us increasingly sensitive toward the dangers involved in excessive impersonality and too much physical presence without communication. What is the effect on a person, already
trying to cope with the pressures mentioned above, of
having to spend a couple hours a day on subways or
buses, and more time on streets and in shops, without
ever receiving a look, word or gesture that indicates
anything beyond cold civility?

No one would suggest that we can establish rules
of thumb to indicate under what circumstances we

should speak to a stranger in public. Yet we appear
to have established an unwritten law that prohibits
communication with strangers under virtually all circumstances. Necessity alone appears to create the
exception. When snow storms (or similar incidents)
create a common crisis in large cities, neighbours of
long standing (who are next to strangers) work together to clear their sidewalks and dig out their
cars. Yet the moment the crisis is over, they return
to the established pattern of not speaking to each
other when they meet on those same sidewalks in the
morning.

Far too frequently we simply tolerate each
other's physical presence, when we could humanize the
situation by the slightest gesture acknowledging each
other. This is depersonalizing, because physical
presence without personal communication causes feelings of rejection and alienation. Experiences of
rejection and lack of openness on the part of individuals are easily rationalized by the recipient; as
a result, the rejected person can become alienated
from society as a whole. How frequently we use that
generalized "they" to describe the way we were treated
by one person on the subway on the way home. In doing
so, we unconsciously increase and express our alienation from people in general, not just from particular
individuals. What is of even greater concern is the
fact that physical presence without personal communication often leads to an insecurity that in turn
causes feelings of lack of personal worth and alienation from ourselves. Being ignored and encountering
those who refuse to acknowledge our dignity weakens
our image of ourselves. Then our negative feelings
toward ourselves can readily develop into contempt
and even hatred for ourselves. An excessive amount
of physical presence in our lives, where there should
be personal presence, leads to alienation from ourselves as well as from others.

Alienation, in turn, breeds hostility. Thus,
ultimately, excessive impersonality in society
creates a tendency in us to want to stab back at
those who do not acknowledge our dignity and personal
worth. By deceiving those who have "put us down,"
destroying their property, stealing from them or
lying to them, we experience, at least temporarily, a
feeling of equality, if not superiority. At least
for the moment we are in control; we have the upper
hand. No matter how unreasonable and immoral such

behaviour is objectively, under the circumstances it seems to be meaningful and satisfying. We do not steal petty things from our employer or from the store, simply because we lack the virtue of honesty; nor do we lie and cheat in a million little ways out of real disrespect for truth. The consequences of a lack of personal presence and communication that acknowledges our dignity and value affect all of us in varying degrees. They also motivate a great deal of dishonesty and untruthfulness to the point where, for some people, these can become a way of life.

My primary concern here has simply been to distinguish between physical and personal presence and to show that the former has more far-reaching consequences than we ordinarily recognize. Before moving on to focus on personal presence, let me conclude by extending this discussion to the religious level of thought. If we cut through the accretions and get down to the central meaning attributed to hell, we find that it is a condition in which there is physical presence without any communication with God or other people. It is a state of being totally isolated, irremediably turned in on oneself, yet at the same time experiencing an insatiable need to share and communicate with others. Certainly it is an exaggeration, but it should come as no great surprise, therefore, when we frequently hear our cities and our places of employment described as living hells.

Personal Presence

Having gained some insight into the reality of physical presence and its effects on people, let us turn now to the opposite end of the spectrum and examine personal presence in its fullest sense. It represents the richest, interpersonal communication possible among us, because it involves communication directed toward mutual self-revelation and understanding. In order to illustrate this point I shall distinguish between a dialogue and a discussion, argument or debate. I use the term dialogue to refer to a communication expressed in words and/or actions in which the partners' purpose is to get to understand and appreciate each other more fully. Their attention is focused primarily upon themselves. Although physical presence is not absolutely essential for a successful dialogue, it is a great advantage.

In discussion, argument and debate there is inevitably an element of self-revelation too. Thus, the parties involved are personally present to each other at least to some extent. This is necessarily so, because we cannot express our ideas and opinions without revealing our inner selves. Nevertheless, in an argument or debate the parties' attention is not focused on either the element of mutual self-revelation or on the increased mutual understanding that are occurring. They are personally present to each other in a different way and to a different degree than are the partners in a dialogue. Their concern is centered on the particular matter of discussion or debate.5 Their attitudes and purposes are not essentially those of acceptance and appreciation. On the contrary, they take a critical and evaluative stance as they strive for clarity, precision and effectiveness. Challenge, competition and desire to show one's superiority undoubtedly enter into discussions as well as arguments and debates. Thus, the mode and degree of presence in these encounters are quite different from that of dialogue.

In a dialogue we express or manifest our deepest thoughts and feelings, that is to say, our inner lives. Dialogue is self-revelation. It necessarily implies an element of trust between us, because we do not run the risks involved in revealing our inner selves unless we have confidence that the recipient will welcome and appreciate what they have to offer. As one partner manifests her/himself, the other shares in her/his very life and self. What the one shares becomes part of the world and life of the other. Thus, the latter participates in the very being of the former. When this sharing is mutual, and only then, is a communion of life established between them.

The encounter we are describing here as personal presence in its fullest sense is a turning and an opening of our very being to each other. We meet each other in our full, personal existence, and make ourselves present to each other as much as that is possible at any moment. Undoubtedly only particular facets of our personalities are revealed at any one time. Nevertheless, we perceive each other and are present to each other in our wholeness and uniqueness. There is a fundamental difference, therefore, to be noted between the mode of presence of partners in a dialogue and that of parties in a debate. In fact, I have deliberately selected the words partners and parties to help convey this distinction.

When we are fully present to each other, our mutual openness and acceptance amounts to a mutual acceptance or confirmation of each other in our very being, as far as this is possible. Such a confirmation is not meant to imply an acceptance or approval of every aspect of each other's personalities. Differences and points of tension will remain. Yet in our willingness to participate in each other's inner lives, we affirm each other as persons.[6] In fact, we must go further than this. We indicated earlier that personhood does not exist prior to or apart from our concrete relations with each other. We come to know ourselves, that is to say, discover who we are at the same time as we create ourselves by revealing ourselves to others. Mutual self-revelation is also mutual self-discovery.[7] In the mutual self-revelation that occurs with our friends, we become ourselves and come to know ourselves. That is, we develop and discover ourselves both through the giving and receiving and the successes and failures that constitute our daily interactions.

I cannot stress too frequently that the communication involved in personal presence extends far beyond the spoken word to include all the symbolic gestures and actions involved in sharing each other's lives. From the point of view of content, some communications are dominantly intellectual (sharing our ideas) and others are dominantly emotional (surrendering or giving ourselves in love). Yet the intellectual and emotional are far more closely interrelated than we often acknowledge. Both have as their primary function to render being present to being--to render people present to each other.

Too frequently we conceive of the knowing process simply as grasping ideas or acquiring facts for useful purposes. Yet knowing is a central mode of rendering things and people present to and in the knower. When I come to know a thing, that thing becomes present to my mind. From then on, it is present in me in the intentional mode of being, influencing me and making me become more a person. When my friends share their ideas, values and what really

matters to them with me, their ideas, values and concerns also enter me and become part of my personality
structure. Through sharing with them, I acquire certain dimensions of their personalities. There is a
sense, then, in which I become part of my friends and
they become part of me. When a friend's deepest concerns become my concerns, not only because I recognize them as good and important, but also because
they are her/his concerns, they become symbols that
mediate or render her/his person present to and in
me. Because values, ideas and concerns are at the
core of our personalities, sharing them is one of the
central means by which we are present to and influence each other.

When we look at mutual self-revelation as a gift
of self to another, we see that self-revelation is an
act of love rendering us present to and in each
other, uniting us and yet allowing us to remain distinct. Volumes have been written on the ways we are
united through love. I shall restrict my comments to
a few central themes that make evident the immediacy
and uniqueness of the presence love enables us to
achieve.

Love is a movement that takes us out beyond the
confines of our own selves to seek union with the
good of another. Love always seeks union with the
good or with something under the guise of a good.
The lover sees a good in the beloved, whether this be
physical appearance, personality or whatever, and
strives to unite her/himself with that goodness.
This attraction or movement is complex. The lover
sees the beloved both as good in herself and as good
for himself. In other words, on the one hand, he
seeks union with the beloved, simply because of the
intrinsic good and value of the beloved in and for
herself. On the other hand, he pursues her, because
union with her intrinsic goodness will result in good
for himself. We can express this double movement by
saying that love is both altruistic and egoistic, a
giving and a possessing. Both elements are present
in love; but the more mature and genuine the love,
the more the possessiveness is subordinated to and
incorporated within the larger movement of giving.
Without the element of giving, there is no love.
Real love, like life itself, is union and sharing.
Where either one of the partners simply tries to appropriate what is given by the other, there is really
no love or shared life between them.

A number of fundamental facts flow directly from what we have said regarding the type of presence created by love. The parties are inwardly and directly present to each other. Gabriel Marcel expresses this fact by saying that the "inward realization of presence through love...exists in an immediacy beyond all conceivable mediation."[8] By this he intends to distinguish the way lovers are present to each other from the presence achieved between those who come together on behalf of a common cause or interest. When we come together to promote a good to which we are individually committed, we certainly enter into each other's presence and begin to share each other's lives. This sharing may become very intense, but it is a mediated presence, one which was originally fostered and is maintained by the mediating attraction of our common concern. The cause we espouse acts as a mediator; it is a unitive force binding us together and promoting the sharing that occurs between us. In time, if we come to know and love each other, this mediating attraction may well remain, but it will be complemented and engulfed by the direct, unitive attraction of love, which will bring us together much more intimately for the sole purpose of living in and enjoying each other's presence.

When we are immediately present to each other in love, we do not simply recognize each other as equals, nor simply acknowledge the rights and claims made upon each other's time and energy. In love we not only recognize, but identify with the very person of our beloved. Her/his rights and claims are not simply acknowledged, but are made our own.[9] The two of us become partners in the fullest possible sense--two who are one, yet remain distinct. Our intimate presence in each other gives us an entirely different stance toward each other than we would take toward a less intimate friend or a party with whom we entered a business contract. Our mutual presence affirms our intrinsic value and dignity as people. Each of us loves the other because of who s/he is, not because of what s/he can accomplish. Thus, neither of us has to strive constantly to prove her/his value as a person. What each of us accomplishes is of value and has meaning to the other, not so much because of its intrinsic worth, but because of who accomplished it.

In the light of what I have just said regarding the union and self-affirmation that occur when lovers

are present to each other, let me comment once again
on the need of a healthy love of self, because it is
so intimately related to personal presence. If we do
not love ourselves in our own life situation with all
our strengths, weaknesses and limited potentialities
(not merely in an idealized one), we cannot be at one
with ourselves. That union with our own being that
should integrate and strengthen us is lacking. We
cannot affirm ourselves nor find satisfaction in ourselves. We are not present to ourselves as who and
what we are. Thus, we must constantly try to be and
to present ourselves as something other than who we
are. We must constantly try to achieve success in
order to prove our own personal worth to ourselves
and to purchase or win the love of others.

Because some of us do not love ourselves, we cannot give of ourselves to others, and therefore are
confirmed in our own low image of ourselves when
others do not respond to us with love. Our inability
to be truly present to ourselves leads to a deep,
pervasive dishonesty at the core of our very existence. We are not true to our own selves, and con-
sequently much of our behaviour is affected by our
lack of self-love. We can appreciate why this is so
if we recall, once again, that personhood is achieved
by entering into satisfying personal relations. To
refuse to enter into mutual relations of friendship
and love is to completely frustrate our existence.
To be limited in our ability to do so, because of
lack of love of self, is to face constant frustration
in all our relationships and, undoubtedly, a high
degree of failure in our most intimate friendships.

We have seen that both knowing and loving create
union by rendering us present to each another.
Healthy self-love enables us to affirm ourselves, and
so be present to ourselves in a creative way that
liberates us to unite with each other. The mutual
love of friends renders them directly or immediately
present to each other. Of course, their mutual pre--
sence is also mediated in other ways, especially
through common interests; but the point I wish to
emphasize here is the immediate, unmediated presence
created by love. This is most significant, because
it is the deepest form of communion or participation
in the life of another that is possible.

Everything I have said so far regarding personal
presence stresses that the union it creates enables

the partners to become themselves at the same time
they influence each other. Yet a moment's reflection
on this point leads me to ask if the mutual presence
of lovers is really an unmixed blessing. Is there
not grave danger that their individual identities
will be lost and that their personalities will be
dissolved in the relationship rather than enriched by
it? Yes, this danger is real. People are present to
each other in some friendships and love relationships
in such a way that they are injured as persons. This
should not be so, but it happens. Before discussing
the deficiencies in these relationships, let me show
why such destructive tendencies are the exception and
not the rule.

Falling in love does not entail losing my self,
but losing my isolated self. Love begins with a meeting or encounter with another person, someone other
than myself. It is precisely the discovery of the
other person, as other, that makes love ecstatic. As
partners we lose only our isolated selves, our isolated identities, because now we find our own selves
or identities accepted and reflected back to us in
the person of the other. The self of each of us remains distinct, not as an isolated, but as a related,
accepted and affirmed self. Therefore, the union
achieved by our love entails an intensified and very
enjoyable awareness of both the uniqueness of myself
and the otherness of my partner. This effects an
enrichment, not a diminishment, of myself. We have
all seen this enrichment in the joy, the satisfaction
and the added vitality reflected in the faces of
lovers.

In a loving relationship, the partners' mutual
knowledge of each other exceeds that of mere facts.
They have an intuitive grasp or knowledge of each
other's very person, a knowledge that accompanies
love and is not directly communicable in language.
Because they know each other so well, and because
they accept and affirm each other in a relationship
to which they are willingly committed, each can afford to be her/himself to the maximum. Where love is
genuine, union differentiates. In fact, union personalizes through differentiating.[10]

That is to say, in an intimate, love relationship, where the partners are as fully present to each
other as possible, there is a deep union, but also
independence and a distance between them.[11] Be-

cause they realize that they are known and accepted for who they are, they feel free to be themselves and to stand by and express their own convictions and opinions. Because their differences are not a threat to their union, they experience themselves as distinct, personal centres. Their relationship normally gives them the freedom to say what they mean and mean what they say. Thus, each partner is able to be truly present to both her/himself and to the other without affectation or role playing. Therefore, we can say that love differentiates, because it gives lovers the distance or space they need, not only to accept their differences, but even to let them develop within reasonable bounds.

Where the distance and independence about which I have spoken is maintained within an intimate, love relationship, there is a maximum of presence and also a maximum of influence and mutual shaping of each other's personalities. Yet neither partner is absorbed--there is no imposing or manipulating. What each reveals of her/himself is genuine, and each is present to the other as who s/he is. The partners' love binds them to each other, yet at the same time makes them free. Genuine love binds, but never coerces. In fact, the opposite is the case. Love creates freedom; where there is no love, there can be no freedom. Where there is only a minimum of love, there is usually coercion. A husband who genuinely loves his wife and children above other things freely cashes his cheque and sets about buying the groceries and paying the rent. A husband who finds his love for a big car or time with the boys or at the track in competition with his love for his wife and children experiences himself as at least somewhat enslaved and coerced.

C.H. Dodd ties together the central themes we have been discussing here, when he says that love is the only relationship in which perfect, social unity co-exists with the utmost freedom of each partner. Only where there is love can we be completely ourselves, while at the same time overcoming our separateness in a common life. As a consequence, in the community we form, there is maximum sharing of life that elevates our individual existence to the status of real personality.[12] It is in this context of sharing life that genuine development of personality is at its maximum. Love unites, differentiates and personalizes. Without love and sharing, life is re-

duced to mere existence. Later, when we examine the
mode of presence involved in functional relationships
and the effect that an over-emphasis on them has on
honesty and truthfulness, the full bearing of these
insights will become more evident.

In spite of what I have been saying about love, I
have already acknowledged that some intimate relationships are destructive of those involved. Our daily
experience makes it clear that the most important
thing in life--genuine, personal love for its own
sake--is missing in many people's lives. We constantly see the numerous, inadequate substitutes that
some accept for love. If love is to be personalizing, the partners must be present to each other as
persons. Far too often this is not the case. For
instance, where love of the other for her/his own
sake is not mutual, where the gift of self is one way
and where love is almost exclusively possessive, the
partners are not mutually present to each other as
personal centres. Their presence to each other is
more like that of objects than that of people.

In some situations, whether consciously or unconsciously, one partner is reduced to an object that
enables the other to overcome loneliness, inadequacy
or insecurity. In other situations, one may be reduced to either an object from which the other receives gratification and the fulfillment of personal
needs, or to an object to which the other can give
her/himself or on which to spend her/his energy. All
these relationships are certainly functional, and
they may even appear to be helpful for a time; but
they are really inadequate, destructive ways of being
present to another person. When the need for which
they were entered into disappears or is fulfilled in
another way, they collapse and the partners are left
feeling cheated and used. In similar instances, when
the superficial rather than the genuine, or the physical, apart from the personal, is the dominant source
of attraction, the relationship tends to turn one or
both the partners back in on themselves, so that they
drift apart rather than achieve unity. The result is
frequently alienation, even from oneself. It is not
difficult to understand why alienation comes about in
any of these situations, because right from the beginning, the partners were never fully present to
each other as people.

In relationships where the partners neither ac-

cept each other as equals nor identify with each
other's rights, one or both their personalities is
stifled. A wife whose equality is denied is possessed by her husband, rather than appreciated. She
is not given the independence and distance necessary
to form and express opinions and to weigh and resist
values that are alien to her own value system. Thus,
she is not allowed to emerge as a person through her
daily interactions.

In order to grow as people, we must derive meanings and form value judgments from our daily encounters. As we mature, we build up a consistent, integrated picture of reality. Since we constantly encounter ideas and values that are inconsistent with
our own, we are continually forced to re-evaluate and
extend our horizons. Thus, all of us are faced with
a twofold problem: maintaining our own inner harmony
or integrity and at the same time maintaining an ongoing harmony with our loved ones and our physical
and social environments.[13] Where close friends and
marriage partners are not really present to one another as people, they do not help each other to develop an integral self-image, nor do they support
each other in facing the tensions and risks involved
in experiencing change and novelty. In fact, in personal relationships that are based primarily on
either possessiveness or the fulfillment of needs,
the very presence of the one to the other blocks the
normal flow of experiences that structure one's self-
awareness and lead to a mature self-identity. Without doing so deliberately, the parties prevent each
other from developing as distinct, mature people with
the result that, inevitably, the uniqueness of one or
both is absorbed or smothered.

For an intimate relationship to be healthy, the
mutual sharing that occurs must be a source of personal growth for both the partners. They must be present to each other in such a way that one gains as
much advantage from the interaction as the other. In
fact, when the partners really complement each other,
the benefits gained by each are distinct. Love certainly entails dying to one's self-centeredness and
becoming detached from one's own needs and interests.
Nevertheless, it does not entail annihilating one's
self or becoming detached from one's own personal
centre. That is to say, it is outrightly erroneous
to think of love as forgetting one's self for the
sake of the other. Such an attitude is destructive of

self and simply dissolves personal relationships,
because it destroys mutuality. A mutual relationship requires that there be two distinct, unique
selves interacting with each other. Therefore, personal presence in the fullest sense requires concern
for oneself and wanting to be oneself in relation to
the other person, for the sake of both oneself and
one's partner distinctly.[14]

What we have just said here does not imply that
either love or personal presence can be achieved without openness, sacrifice, suffering and a great deal
of effort. Where distinct advantages for each partner are to be achieved, a maximum of listening, sensitivity, passivity (allowing oneself to be acted upon)
and adaptability are required of each. Furthermore,
in a relationship where these virtures are practised,
the presence achieved will be radically different
from, and much more demanding than, that in a relationship based on defacement of self for the other.

It is evident from what we have been saying that
personal presence is neither a purely objective nor a
purely subjective reality. Presence is certainly
objective; it cannot exist without real people being
present to each other. It is an interpersonal or
interhuman reality, yet not something that exists or
stands by itself as a distinct entity. One person is
present to and in another. Therefore, since it is an
attribute of a person, an influx of one person into
another, there is a genuine objectivity about it.

On the other hand, presence is also a subjective
reality, because a person can only be present to another according to the capacity of the latter to be
open to and receive that presence. The subjective
element in personal presence, like that in any form
of communication or sharing, is essential; but it is
only a part of the whole reality. Where we reveal
ourselves to each other as we are, there is an authenticity and objectivity to our presence which can best
be described in terms of relational objectivity.
Thus, we can see that genuine presence is intimately
connected with being honest with ourselves and truthful in presenting ourselves as we really are. It is
not surprising, therefore, to find that Gabriel
Marcel sees a very close connection between personal
presence and what he describes as creative fidelity.[15] His analysis of the relation between personal presence and availability also adds another

dimension to what we have been saying. It highlights the fact that the distinction between presence and absence is not the same as that between attention and distraction, as is illustrated in the following example.

Let us suppose that I am in pain and in need of confiding in someone. Two friends show their interest and good will by giving me their attention. One gives me the feeling of really being present or at my disposal, while the other does not. The latter is very conscientious about what s/he is doing, and is most willing to offer her/his time, energy and material favours. Yet this second friend is incapable of making room for me in her/himself. This person's way of listening is not a way of giving her/himself, but ultimately a way of refusing this gift. Thus, this friend's visible action or limited gift does not witness to her/his full personal presence to me. The other friend, who is genuinely at my disposal, is capable of being with me with the whole of her/himself while my need exists. S/he conveys this presence immediately and unmistakably in a look, smile, tone of voice or other gesture. For the one I am an object, one with needs that require attention; and s/he offers me what s/he can out of her/his abundance. For the other I am a presence, and s/he immediately makes her/himself fully present to me in return.[16]

In the one case a reciprocal relationship, a communion, is established between myself and my friend. In the other, this communion is limited or even lacking. In spite of good will and actual efforts, the absence of communion between us seriously restricts this friend's ability to help me. As well, the absence of a presence or communion, that should exist between us, also has a tremendous effect on the degree of honesty with which I can reveal my pain and the degree of truthfulness and candor with which I can unburden what I need to confide. Once again, therefore, we see how complex the reality of personal presence is and how it effects our ability to communicate or share where and what we really are. We frequently conceal more than we reveal, and this is inevitably in direct proportion to the degree of personal presence that exists between us.

Let us look a bit further at the tremendous influence we have on each other for better or for worse

through our presence. When I am present to you, you
take on part of my very being, become to some extent
(like) me by sharing my feelings, ideas and ultimate
concerns. I am present with and in you in my absence,
and even after my death, because my influence has
been internalized and lives on as part of you. Obviously, then, there is a sense in which my reality
or person is not entirely contained or restricted
within the dimensions of my physical body. It extends to every person and place where my influence is
felt and internalized. Through our ongoing interactions with each other, our body-persons are literally
made out of each other. Yet, in this process, no one
need lose her/his own personality or identity.

Working with this same Whiteheadian concept of
presence, Bernard Lee analyzes the mutual interaction
and influence of a society on its members and the
members on the society. He even shows, rather con-
vincingly, that this approach to presence corresponds
rather closely to the concept of Jesus' presence in
the Christian community understood as the Body of
Christ. In becoming a member of any society, whether
secular or religious, we internalize or embody in our
own lives its defining characteristics. Then we propagate the life of the society to other members and to
outsiders. That is, the life of the society is first
internalized and made present in us. Then, since its
dominant concerns and defining characteris- tics have
become part of us, we present them through our
interactions to all those we encounter.[17]

Most of us belong to a number of organizations,
the characteristics and values of which are varied
and not always complementary or even compatible. We
see, then, that at any moment in our lives we are
confronted with a multiplicity of values and concerns
competing for our attention. Each one we decide to
internalize influences us by orienting our development in a particular direction. Thus, we get a
glimpse of the ethical consequences inherent in the
choices we make regarding personal presence. We
shall certainly have to examine these consequences in
relation to honesty and truthfulness. However, we
shall not do this until we have gained an understanding of presence in its functional mode.

These observations pretty well conclude my initial, explanatory discussion of personal presence.
By way of summarizing the central points I have made,

I shall turn briefly to the thought of George Tavard. In an article on the presence of God, written from the perspective of biblical theology, he sums up the characteristics of the divine presence to us. It is interesting to note that the conclusions Tavard and I draw from our own individual perspectives are fundamentally indistinguishable.

First, personal presence is a phenomenon of life, a spiritual phenomenon that implies an active relationship with another person. It cannot be equated with physical location, because the latter is limited and measurable, whereas presence is not. Physical presence assists, but is not absolutely essential to personal presence. Because it is spiritual, presence is virtually universal. Nevertheless, we direct our presence to one person or another by choice. Since being present to another is a matter of choice, personal presence is inseparable from love and freedom. Although it is not always recognized, at some point in the process of falling in love, a lover makes a free choice to enter into an intimate union with and to be fully present to her/his beloved. Since personal presence implies the possibility of making oneself present to another or not, it also implies both the freedom to transcend the location of one's presence and the possibility of withdrawing it. Because presence is a spiritual phenomenon, it is also a means of communication. Its purpose is to enable us to communicate or share, not only our ideas and feelings, but our very being. If this communication is to be effective, however, those offered it must be willing to accept what is offered and to reciprocate by also choosing to be present in the same way. Thus, presence is always an actual or vital relationship, and one that requires a mutual response made in fidelity and with commitment.[8]

Notes

1. For a detailed explanation of my understanding of the processive nature of reality, see the first five chapters of my earlier work entitled, *A Processive World View for Pragmatic Christians* (New York: Philosophical Library, Publishers, 1975), pp. 1-136.
2. For the fundamental concept of presence, set forth here, I am indebted to the thought of Alfred

North Whitehead, who states that his "philosophy of organism is mainly devoted to the task of making clear the notion of 'being present in another entity.'" *Process and Reality* (New York: The Free Press, 1969), p. 65.

3. John Cowburn, *Love and the Person* (London: Geoffrey Chapman, 1967), pp. 107-08.

4. For a discussion of the role of emotions in the creation of presence in a very different context, see Bernard Lee, *The Becoming of the Church* (New York: Paulist Press, 1974), pp. 118, 227-28.

5. Cowburn, pp. 107-08.

6. Martin Buber, "Elements of the Interhuman," *The Knowledge of Man*, trans. by M. Friedman and R. G. Smith (London: George Allen & Unwin Ltd., 1965), p. 85.

7. Macmurray, p. 170.

8. Gabriel Marcel, *The Philosophy of Existence*, trans. by Manya Harari (New York: Philosophical Library, Publishers, 1949), p. 6.

9. Emil Brunner, *The Divine Imperative, A Study in Christian Ethics*, trans. by Olive Wyon (New York: Macmillan Co., 1937), p. 326.

10. Culliton, p. 200.

11. A number of authors who focus on people as relational beings discuss the distance and independence that exist within genuine, personal relationships: M. Buber, "Distance and Relation," *The Knowledge of Man*, pp. 59-71, 117; C. Moustakas, *Loneliness and Love*, p. 67; Marc Oraison, *Being Together: Our Relationships with Other People*, trans. by Rosemary Sheed (Garden City, New York: Doubleday Image Books, 1971), pp. 42-43.

12. C. H. Dodd, *New Testament Studies* (Manchester: Manchester University Press, 1967), p. 155.

13. Prescott Lecky, "The Personality," *The Self: Explorations in Personal Growth*, ed. by Clarke E. Moustakas (New York: Harper & Row, 1956), pp. 89-92.

14. Oraison, p. 114.

15. Marcel, pp. 21-25.

16. Ibid., pp. 25-26.

17. George H. Tavard, *The Presence of God* (New York: Paulist Press, Pamphlet Series, 1965), pp. 4-5.

18. Lee, pp. 152-53; 178-79.

Chapter 3

THE FUNCTIONAL MODE OF PRESENCE

Impersonal Relations, Attitudes and Knowledge

From the very beginning, I have insisted that a person is a being-in-relation. That is to say, as individuals we exist in personal relation to one another, not in isolation. In and through my relationships I am constituted an "I" or person in my own concrete existence. Nevertheless, within a relationship, one or both of us can intentionally isolate ourselves from each other, so that the relationship becomes impersonal. Thus, relationships may be either personal or impersonal, and knowledge of others may also be either personal or impersonal. On the one hand, personal relations constitute us as people, and we acquire personal knowledge of others only by entering into a personal relationship with them. On the other hand, we can enter into impersonal relationships, when we deliberately isolate ourselves from each other by intention. In this situation, we obtain a valid, genuine knowledge of each other. However, it is an objective knowledge, a knowledge of the other as an object in the world, not a knowledge of the other in personal relation to us.

Impersonal knowledge is based on observation and inference. It is an abstract knowledge arrived at by limiting our attention to what can be known about another person without entering into a personal relation with her/him. Personal and impersonal (objective) knowledge are distinguished, therefore, because the latter is knowledge of matter of fact only. It necessarily excludes any knowledge of what is a matter of intention.[1]

John Macmurray's thought on this topic is very

insightful. He maintains that we can regard each other as objects. Because the personal is more extensive and more fundamental than the impersonal, it includes its own negative. This is to say that impersonality is, in reality, simply the negative aspect of the personal. Only people can act impersonally.[2] Thus, personal relations and personal knowledge include their own negative in the form of impersonal relations and impersonal knowledge. To understand this correctly, it must be absolutely clear that when we refer to impersonal relations and knowledge as the negative aspect of the personal, we do not intend to deny their positive content and value. If you and I are friends, and therefore live in a personal relationship with each other, we have both a personal and a purely factual knowledge of each other. We live in a relatively intimate, mutual, personal presence, one that at least approximates what we have described as personal presence in its fullest sense. Thus, the impersonal, objective knowledge we have of each other is not isolated, but seen within the larger, richer context of our mutual presence.

In impersonal relationships we establish a very different presence from that which we would have achieved had we not negated the personal. However, our presence to each other is not merely physical. We are people in communication with each other, but for some reason we have intentionally avoided a deep, personal relationship. Since we do not have a personal knowledge of each other, the impersonal or factual knowledge we acquire of each other stands alone. Thus, I want to emphasize, once again, that the term negative is used here simply to indicate that in impersonal relations the larger, personal context has been intentionally negated or avoided. The factual knowledge that we acquire is grasped in isolation from the deeper, personal presence and knowledge that would ordinarily include it. Nevertheless, impersonal knowledge is good, valid knowledge. I cannot emphasize too much, therefore, that it is wrong to associate pejorative connotations with an understanding of the impersonal as the negation of the personal.

As I have already implied, in a personal relationship, we necessarily amass a considerable body of objectively known facts about each other. In a limited sense, therefore, we know each other as objects, in spite of the fact that we maintain a personal relationship. In fact, the knowledge we gain of other people with whom we live in personal relations, if developed, gives us a personal, common sense understanding of people in general. The impersonal knowledge we amass, if it is systematically pursued, gives rise to scientific knowledge of people. These bodies of knowledge are very different, but both are necessary and complementary.

Let us begin now to tie together what we said in the first two chapters about personal presence and what we are saying here about personal and impersonal relations and knowledge. From the perspective of personal presence, we have already seen that we realize ourselves most directly and fully in intimate, personal relations of knowing and loving. In performing these acts, we are carrying out our most creative, peak experiences, exercising our most personal, rewarding activities and fulfilling our highest aspirations. We have also seen that because we are meant to live in intimate fellowship with each other, our acts of knowing, loving and enjoying each other are performed simply for their own sake. These acts, which, of course, include acts of personal knowledge as described here, are ends in themselves, not means to other goals. Therefore, they need no justification. They are neither secondary, incidental acts that we perform, nor acts which should be subordinated to less direct or less perfect, impersonal interactions. Thus, our personal relations and our personal, non-scientific knowledge of each other are that without which we cannot become ourselves. They do not require or admit of any form of justification. They are justified in and of themselves.

On the other hand, impersonal relations and impersonal knowledge are the negation of the personal. When we see them in this larger, personal context, we can readily see that they are neither the ideal nor the norm. Limiting our interactions to impersonal relations and knowledge is not automatically or unconditionally justifiable. In fact, such limitations are justifiable only insofar as our impersonal behaviour is oriented toward and necessary for fostering the personal. An impersonal relation is justified by a relation to a personal intention which includes it as its negative. If it has no such relation or is not controlled in such a manner, it is not justifiable.[3] The ramifications of these conclusions will become more evident when we explain the functional nature of the impersonal and the functional mode of presence.

For the moment, it is sufficient to realize that these conclusions reverse popular opinion and practice. Our constant error in this respect is to regard the impersonal as an end in itself. We forget that impersonal relations are the negative of something richer and more rewarding than themselves. Thus, we justify them automatically. So too, we regard impersonal, objective and scientific knowledge as the complete account of what it is to be human. We forget that it is relative; thus, we absolutize it. In our society, this procedure amounts to a rather widespread rejection of that personal knowledge that accompanies love and the freedom and intuitive grasp of truth it entails. We fail to understand the limited, but special quality of scientific knowledge, with the result that we make the objective the norm for all knowledge and all attitudes.[4]

Let us move one step further by extending what we have been saying to an analysis of personal and impersonal attitudes and the knowledge associated with them. The attempt to maintain an impersonal attitude toward others in many situations is lauded as the only way to see accurately and to arrive at truth. Nevertheless, once again, we propose that an impersonal attitude is also a negative that ought ordinarily to be included within a more extensive, personal attitude. If at times we allow our impersonal observations and attitudes to dominate our relationships, we see the acts and hear the words people speak, but we do not necessarily apprehend their real intentions and feelings through these words and gestures. In brief, we are in danger of missing the meaning of what they are saying or doing.

Our ordinary procedure for getting to know people is a very active process characterized far more by attitudes that are impersonal and functional than by a more personal attitude of receptivity. When our attitude toward others is impersonal and objective, our knowledge is obtained by operations of categorizing, schematizing, classifying and abstracting from that which they present of themselves to us. What we observe is filtered through our own system of categories, with the result that we don't perceive the full reality of what we encounter. As observers, we shape and select, because we choose what to perceive and what to ignore in terms of the needs, fears, interests and uses we have for those being observed. In ordinary knowledge, the observer tends to abstract, because abstractions are useful. Nevertheless, to the extent that an abstraction is useful, it is also limited, and may even be false. This cannot help but be so, simply because some aspects of the person are overlooked, ignored, exaggerated and/or distorted. Thus, there is a sense in which we, as impersonal knowers, create, manufacture or make the object of our knowledge what we want it to be.[5]

When we arrive at our knowledge of others by the process of abstraction, there is also the problem of relating the qualities we observe in them to our system of language. This is a serious difficulty, because what is often most significant in our knowledge of other people is ineffable and simply cannot be adequately expressed in words.[6] Thus, in order that our ordinary, objective knowledge of others comes closer to being a true knowledge of them, we must attempt to grasp them in their many-faceted concreteness. We can also try to perceive in them what is ineffable and resist the temptation to express this in language. These efforts will complement the ordinary process by which we abstract a limited number of their qualities in terms of the functions, needs or interests that motivated us to get to know them in the first place. Nevertheless, even with these added efforts, impersonal knowledge remains the negative aspect of the personal, and is no substitute for it.

In our analysis of personal presence in its fullest sense, we saw that knowing people as they really are requires a process of dialogue or mutual self-revelation. It goes without saying that the relationship in question here is a personal, not an impersonal one. It is also evident that personal knowledge of another depends, not only on the activity of the knower, but also on that of the person revealing her/himself. If there is no mutual opening of the partners to each other in confidence and love, neither can gain a personal knowledge of the other. Personal communion is a two way street. No one can know another person, if the self-revelation between them, and therefore also the sharing of life, is not mutual.

In fact, as we also saw earlier, self-revelation is at one and the same time self-discovery. I gain a

personal knowledge of myself in and through acts of
revealing myself, receiving the responses of friends
to my self-revelations, and, in turn, accepting their
confidences regarding themselves. Thus, I can never
attain a personal knowledge of myself nor of a friend,
if either of us hides behind a false front, puts on
an act, pretends to accept ideas and values s/he really rejects or simply refrains from revealing her/
himself.[7]

There is also a significant difference between
the knowledge we attain in impersonal relations and
that acquired in peak moments of aesthetic, mystical
and religious experience. In these moments, as well
as in moments of love, things are perceived as a unity. The part is seen momentarily as if it were the
whole. A loved one known in this way retains all the
attributes of the whole of being. This mode of knowing is complete or integral, because it is detached,
disinterested, desireless and unmotivated. When our
vision transcends the realm of use, need and posses-
sion, we perceive people in their uniqueness with
their own, intrinsic qualities intact. By contrast,
in impersonal relations, our knowledge of people is
fragmented and partial, because we concentrate on
facets of their personalities that are of particular
intent to us at the moment. Our emotional response
in peak experiences also gives them a special quality
of reverence, humility and surrender that intensifies
these moments, so we experience both the moment and
the people involved as something great.[8] Ordinarily, this emotional response is lacking in impersonal
encounters.

This discussion of impersonal relations, attitudes and knowledge enables us to see that impersonal
relationships are entered into intentionally for a
specific, functional purpose. In such interactions,
we relate with and appreciate each other for our more
limited capacity as agents (means), rather than as
people (ends in and for ourselves). Especially in
the most extreme forms of impersonal attitudes and
relations, we do not regard each other as complete
persons or as free, responsible agents, but as objects who possess certain desirable abilities and
characteristics that make us good functionaries under
certain circumstances. Our relationships are impersonal, then, when they subordinate the personal to
the impersonal. In such relationships, the negative
dominates and subordinates the positive and the posi-

tive is used for the sake of the negative, not the reverse.[9]

Impersonal relations are functional. They include that whole body of interactions that belong to the realm of using things, fulfilling needs, obtaining possessions and providing services. We have seen that impersonal relations are subordinate to personal ones and that functional relations are impersonal. Therefore, they too ought to be subordinated to that which is personal. Since functional relations are secondary and subordinate to fostering personal life, they should never be regarded as more important than our personal relations or our family life. When they are understood in terms of personal presence, they spread themselves out on the spectrum we discussed above, somewhere between experiences of personal presence in the fullest sense and the least possible degree of personal presence (that next door to mere physical presence). With this background as a foundation, in the next section of this chapter, I shall examine the functional mode of presence in greater depth.

Functional Presence

There is no doubt that most people in our society enter into far more impersonal relationships than personal ones. We keep many, if not most, of our neighbours on an acquaintance level and select only a few business associates to become our personal friends. We are highly, if not overly, socialized, simply because most of us encounter large numbers of people every day in our ordinary interactions. In this milieu, it is not surprising that we have come to conceive of impersonal attitudes, knowledge and relations as the normal way of interacting and personal relationships as deliberate, restricted exceptions. Because we simply don't have time and energy to relate personally with most people we meet, we take it for granted that impersonal relations are an end in themselves and automatically justified. Without doing so deliberately, we subordinate the personal to the impersonal on a rather consistent basis.

In our previous discussion of impersonal attitudes, knowledge and relations, we reversed the relationship between the personal and impersonal. We

established the fact that the former is that which
personalizes us (and so is self-justified), while the
latter is simply its negative aspect. Now, with this
background in mind, we are prepared to discuss functional relations effectively.

Today, we enter into many direct relations with
people with whom we are at least acquainted. We gain
some personal knowledge of each other in these ongoing encounters, and can either develop them into
more personal relationships or allow them to diminish
to a more indirect, impersonal level. We also participate in an extensive network of indirect relations
in which we co-operate with others in some form of
functional capacity. These relations are entered
into intentionally. They are not based on mutual,
personal knowledge, nor are they directed toward a
personal relationship for its own sake. Broadly
speaking, they encompass the economic aspect of our
lives and include our work lives. They are the negative aspect of our direct relationships and of our
personal, social lives in the sense that we enter
into them intentionally and co-operatively, so that
we can produce and distribute the commodities (means)
required to promote the personal lives of all the
members of our society.

Our indirect relations, therefore, are independent of our personal relationships and are their negative aspect. Personal communication in these relations may range from non-existent, through unfriendly,
to positive or even cordial. However, these relations as such remain impersonal. In these indirect,
functional relations we intentionally subordinate the
personal to the impersonal for a set purpose. We
enter these relations not as people in the full sense,
but primarily as workers. In fact, we frequently
abstract the functional aspect of ourselves as workers and refer to it in isolation. By doing so, we
identify ourselves with the useful functions we perform.[10] In a real sense, we reduce the whole to
the part when we say, I am a carpenter, a doctor, a
typist or a mechanic.

There is no doubt that the functional aspect of
the personal (our economic and work lives) is intentional and for the sake of our personal lives. It is
intentional, because we develop and maintain it by
deliberate effort. It is the negative aspect of the
personal and, as such, is directed toward the personal

as its means. Thus, it is not self-justifying. The functional aspect of our personal lives finds its justification by reference to the quality of personal life it makes possible. The functional is primarily utilitarian. Its standard is efficiency. Its goal or aim is to produce the greatest quantity, quality and variety of goods for a given expenditure of labour.

It is evident, therefore, that from the economic point of view, each of us as worker is a potential source of energy to be used as efficiently as possible. We are means to an end--the production of the means of life. Thus, once again, we see why the network of functional relations in our lives has to be evaluated and judged as a whole by the role it plays in promoting the personal lives of all the workers involved. Economic efficiency achieved at the expense of the personal lives of those involved is self-condemned and self-frustrating.[11]

Abuses that promote economic efficiency at the expense of workers are common in many areas of the work world. For instance, companies often demand that full time employees work many hours of overtime, because it is less expensive to pay time and a half for these extra hours than to pay the salaries and fringe benefits involved in hiring other workers. Many people are required to work nights on a regular basis for long periods of time without the opportunity to shift back and forth from day to night work. These demands frequently do serious injury to their personal and family lives. The actual content of many people's work is reduced to that which is so trivial and repetitive that the workers themselves are depersonalized. At times, even today, unsatisfactory working conditions remain to the detriment of the health of workers. These are but a few illustrations of incidents in which the means (efficient economic activity) is given precedence over the end (a high quality of personal life) which, ultimately, work life is meant to promote.

In functional relations, what I do is important, not primarily because it is done by me, as someone who is known and loved; but because I am an agent who performs the function efficiently. In this sense, that aspect of my personality that is worker is distinguished and valued above my whole person. As a worker, I am not directly and primarily accepted,

respected and valued in and for my own being (as an
end), but rather as a means to an end. As worker, I
am analyzed, categorized, organized, manipulated,
shifted, rewarded, overlooked, penalized and summed
up in terms of the functions I am expected to perform
efficiently.

There are also other areas in which the differences between personal and functional relations create serious consequences. In looking at our personal
relationships earlier, we saw that intimacy and personal knowledge create a distance between us that
liberates us to be ourselves to the fullest. Intimacy overcomes uneasiness. Rather than being
threatened by each other, mutual acceptance creates
an atmosphere of personal security in which we can
reveal ourselves freely to each other without fear.
In our functional relationships, there is also a distance between us; but it is quite unlike that in our
intimate, personal relationships. The impersonality
caused because we relate as functionaries, outside a
personal relationship, is the source of this distance
between us. The love that could enable us to know
each other in truth (as we truly are) is missing.
Our knowledge of each other is that limited, partial,
objective knowledge we have already discussed. Thus,
the distance between us in a functional mode of presence is a cause of insecurity. It is the type of
distance that does not enable us to be ourselves and
to know that we are accepted. This distance creates
uneasiness and we readily become a threat to each
other.

The type of knowing that dominates in functional
relationships is abstraction with all its biases and
inaccuracies. Not only workers, but also their foremen, are only too aware that they are being summed up
in terms of their utility and efficiency. Such situations are invariably competitive, and therefore all
the more threatening. Thus, there is a deliberate
effort on the part of everyone concerned to reveal
her/himself only as s/he wants to be seen. Behaviour
is motivated more by fear than by love; and deception,
role playing, and covering up characterize the communication process. It is not uncommon that those
involved move farther and farther from knowing each
other and from honesty and truth as we have defined
them. In fact, as impersonality and competition increase, there is a natural tendency for dishonesty
and lying to increase proportionately, simply in order

that those involved can protect themselves against
each other and against "the system."

It is evident, therefore, that there is a genuine
difference between the mode of presence that is fully
personal and one that is functional. Yet, is there
any reason for drawing a hard and fast line of demar-
cation between the personal and functional? The latter, as impersonal, will remain the negative aspect
of the personal. Nevertheless, this does not prevent
those who relate with each other on a functional
basis from also entering into a personal relationship.
Functional relationships do not require that we deliberately restrict our knowledge to functional knowledge of each other. Nor do functional relationships
justify reducing each other simply to means. As people, we cannot avoid entering into functional relationships in which we are a means to an end. We have
to do so in order to go on living. However, there is
nothing to prevent us from respecting ourselves and
each other as persons at the same time.

We allow ourselves to fall into the grave error
of living and working as if functional relationships
are more important than personal ones and as if our
jobs are more important than our very persons. There
is nothing in the nature of functional relationships
that requires or justifies this popular stance. We
also injure ourselves seriously by allowing ourselves
to be thought of and actually reduced to mere functionaries in our economic and work activities. We
tend to isolate our functional relationships and al-
lot a certain amount of time for them. Then we devote the time that is left over to personal relationships. In a healthy environment, the personal and
functional can and should be integrated.

In one sense, everything I do is functional, because in some way it contributes to the community in
which I live. Yet no activity needs to be exclusively functional. The functional is open to being personal, because I can perform a function as a person
(an end) and not as a mere functionary (a means).
Secondly, my functions themselves can become media or
channels that foster personal interaction, when I
perform them intelligently and with love. Thus, all
my functional activities can be enriched or transformed, so that they contribute to my personal development and to the personal enrichment of those for whom
I work.

In a similar manner, a housewife and mother constantly performs activities that are at one and the
same time necessary functions and very personal acts
of love. A husband and father goes beyond the home
to work. Let us say that his profession is teaching.
This is a very personal activity through which he
achieves his own self-realization, yet one that at
the same time fulfills a necessary, social function.
Nor is the function of eating a meal simply functional. It takes on a whole new meaning when it is a
social activity in which a family shares. One participates in a meal. Thus, these three examples illustrate activities in which, at least in principle, the
personal and functional are intertwined to the point
where they are almost identical.

Nevertheless, we know dozens of mothers who experience their daily housework as depersonalizing
drudgery. We have all met topnotch teachers these
days who have either pulled out of teaching or are
simply trying to hang on. They do not experience
themselves as professional educators, but feel reduced to mere functionaries trying to do the best
they can in an indifferent, if not hostile, environment. We also know how almost impossible it is to
get the family together for a meal even once a week,
and then the participation in anything beyond the
physical eating is so often problematic.

There is little doubt that a major factor in
causing this deterioration is our attitude toward
people themselves. We tend to regard them as existing primarily to perform functions efficiently.
They are more important for what they do than for who
they are in and of themselves. The mother and housewife finds she is taken for granted and reduced to
less than a person in her own home. The teacher
finds s/he cannot teach in a situation that is not
only impersonal, but outrightly threatening. Once
disrespect and impersonality dominate the classroom,
the teaching profession is simply reduced to a tough
job for which one collects one's pay. There is little teaching, and even less learning, accomplished.
Impersonality seems to be permeating family life to
the extent that many homes are reduced to mere houses
in which the members reside. Friction and open hostility are kept at a minimum, so long as the members
perform the ritual and functional acts that are expected of them.

These are some of the drastic consequences that
have occurred, because we have allowed the personal
and functional to be torn asunder and even set off
against each other. When we lose sight of the fundamental truth that we are more important than the
things we produce and the functions we perform, we
distort the truth concerning what it is to be human
and we create an environment that is depersonalizing.
Having seen this, let us develop and qualify even
further what we have said about the functional mode
of presence, by examining the stance we ordinarily
take toward material things and each other in the
mode of presence we assume at work.

The Work Mode of Presence

Work is purposeful activity. When we begin to
work, we set out to accomplish a project; we have a
purpose and a plan. We approach the reality on which
we are going to work with the intention of striving
to mold, shape or alter it in a specific way. Our
entire presence, imagination, will and thought must
be in accord with and at the service of this intention, if we are to succeed. The work mode of presence requires concentration and readiness. It is a
goal-oriented way of existing. As workers, we approach the things and people associated with our jobs
with an analytical, penetrating look, rather than in
a contemplative or appreciative way. We regard them
objectively and impersonally, in order to analyze
them and see which elements of the objects and which
characteristics of the people are of value in relation to our goals. Our approach is critical. We do
not view reality in a restful way as something in
itself, but as a means, as something to be worked on
in order to produce something else.[12]

The work mode of presence is obviously a thought-
ful way of relating to reality. Thought is essential
to and characteristic of work. When we are forced to
perform functions that do not require thought, these
functions dehumanize us. To be authentic, the activity to be performed must be capable of retaining our
attention. In fact, in work, our attention is ordinarily concentrated and directed. Our senses are
selectively attuned and our whole person is present
in a specialized way that is characterized by aggressiveness. Matter resists change and formation. Thus,

the worker must face this resistance as something to
be overcome. To succeed at work we must be more aggressive than passive, more grasping than receptive.

As workers, we act as free agents, yet no agent
is free without limits. The nature and inherent laws
of the matter on which we work or the job we are doing
imposes fundamental limits on our freedom. These
limitations form the framework within which we are
free to conceive and foster change. We are not able
to shape or control reality in any way we desire,
simply because matter is restrictive and resistive.
There is a sense, therefore, in which, as workers, we
must be willing to adapt our plans and activities to
the laws of the materials to be used. Nevertheless,
this does not alter the fact that the mood and intention characteristic of the work mode of presence is a
determination to dominate and control.[13]

As workers we must also have power to accomplish
what we set out to do. We must be free to appropriate, use and manipulate reality for our own purposes.
We must achieve a sense of satisfaction from the work
itself, if we are to be motivated to continue committing ourselves to it. There is a considerable amount
of emotion related to work because our vested interests are at stake. Experiences of resistance and
frustration, as well as possibilities of success or
failure, make our involvement in work an emotional
one. In fact, the extent to which our work arouses
emotion is an index of the extent to which it involves us in the world. Psychologically, flight from
work is indicative of escape from the world. On the
other hand, when we are genuinely involved in work,
there is a sense in which, as worker, we live to fin-
ish the project. The activity of each moment on the
job finds its full meaning in terms of the completion
yet to be achieved.[14]

It is evident that during work we are not present
to the world of people and things in the same way we
are during other experiences. We know intuitively
that during leisure and when expressing love our presence to others is different from that during work.
The difference may be summed up as that between striving and non-striving or that between "make it be" and
"let it be" attitudes and activities.

The attitudes and moods that constitute the work
stance toward reality are only some of the attitudes

of which we are capable. We bring our whole personalities or selves to work, so that attitudes that characterize work can never be totally isolated in us
from our other attitudes. This is to say that during
work, attitudes characteristic of the shaping presence are in the forefront. They take precedence over
more caring, respectful and receptive attitudes.
However, they ought never to dominate to the exclusion of these other attitudes. The work mode of presence, if it is totalized and allowed to obliterate
our more receptive attitudes toward people and things,
is not a fully human mode of presence. Aggressiveness, dominance and the will to control are forceful
attitudes which can easily overpower our more receptive qualities. If and when this occurs, our development as people is injured and even our work may become less than human.[15]

The attitudes that characterize us as agents or
workers are necessarily present in us while at work.
Yet they need not be the only attitudes that are present. As workers, we do not have to be less caring
and respectful during work than outside of it. When
working, we must be present in a specialized work
mode. Nevertheless, if the atmosphere of work is to
remain personal and humanizing, we must integrate
other attitudes and qualities within the more aggressive, "make it happen" stance toward reality.[16]

An unlimited power over people or things is destructive of all concerned. It isolates, causes loneliness and becomes self-defeating. In order to avoid
dehumanizing ourselves, we must direct the power we
appropriate toward action and direct our actions toward service. In this context, the power at our disposal is limited and related to other values, and not
used simply for our own advantage. Our capacity to
grasp onto reality for our own ends can lead to a
world that is so centered around ourselves that it
becomes empty. Besides appropriating and shaping, we
must respect and let be or we soon lose sight of the
meaning of our activities in relation to the lives
and activities of others.

The satisfaction we receive from our work can
also be turned in on ourselves in a destructive manner, if it is not balanced by generosity and acceptance of the suffering that is inherent in creative
activity. The attitudes and mood, as well as the
dynamics that operate in the work situation, must

also be balanced and harmonized with those other
attitudes and dynamics that come to the fore in moments of friendship and full, personal presence.
These two sets of attitudes and dynamics complement
each other. If work attitudes are not moderated, we
risk the danger of dehumanizing ourselves and our
work; and unfavourable consequences soon permeate
every facet of our lives.[17] In fact, it is possible to approach every aspect of life as a project or
a piece of work. When we allow this to happen, our
experience is reduced to the single experience of
work, in spite of the fact that we are performing
activities that are not work. Ordinarily, when we
love, play and pray, we are present to and experience
each other in a very different way from our experience of each other during work. The various modes by
which we are present to each other during these ac-
tivites are meant to give variety and enrichment to
our experience.

When the work mode of presence unconsciously dominates our lives, all our experiences and activities
become projects. Our intentions and perspective become narrow and fixated, and our very lives are reduced to something much less creative, varied and
rewarding than they are meant to be.[18] The detrimental consequences that result from reducing ourselves to the status of workers are far-reaching.
When work becomes our central experience of reality,
we tend to appreciate only values that are related to
productivity. We estimate our own, personal value
almost entirely in terms of what we can or cannot
accomplish successfully; and we lose sight of our
personal worth apart from what we do. The result of
this perspective, of course, is a very deep, pervasive insecurity. Success is not won with ease, and
so often it depends upon factors beyond our control.
Thus, we have to work harder to ensure it, and ensure
it we must, because our self-respect and self-esteem
depend upon it. Our value as people is constantly
threatened, so we feel driven or compelled to bolster
it up and re-construct it.

Those among us who have allowed themselves to be
reduced to workers live as if their very being in and
of itself is valueless. Because they are compulsively driven from within, it is almost impossible
for them to relax or take their time. They are always
restless and in a hurry. They think in terms of the
analytical and useful. Life has become one great

series of projects that require planning.[19] Those who are locked into the work mode of presence are really present neither to themselves nor to others. They are never truly present to themselves, because they simply deny or repress much of themselves. They are not in touch with their own feelings and do not know, love or value themselves as they really are. Nor are they really present to other people, because they cannot see and value them in their integrity. They screen out and do not appreciate anything but the useful and what is compatible with the work mode of presence. Even then, such people are rarely fully present to the people with whom they are conversing at any moment, because they always tend to be one step removed, analyzing the situation or planning the next move or the next sentence.

The lives of people who are locked into the work mode of presence are characterized by a fundamental and all-pervasive lack of honesty and truthfulness as we have defined them. They are neither truly present to themselves nor to others. Even if they are scrupulous about speaking the truth and acting honestly, these qualities do not permeate their lives. They cannot afford to reveal themselves as they are, even if they know themselves well enough to do so. Those facts or truths about themselves that they choose to reveal are selected and presented in such a way that they misrepresent their real selves, even if each isolated fact is perfectly accurate. Their actions are so purposeful and restricted that they conceal far more than they reveal about their real personalities. Their whole self is deliberately concealed in even their most personal relationships.

It is also very difficult for such people to develop the virtues of honesty and truthfulness, because their insecurity leaves them constantly threatened. Because they cannot love themselves as they are, they experience an exaggerated, psychological need for success in order to maintain their self-respect. Thus, they are tempted to misrepresent the facts, to lie and to cheat in order to gain the success they need. Eventually they seé this behaviour as normal and acceptable, because as they understand reality, this is what a person has to do to survive.

When we regard success as the standard of personal value, we tend to deny our failures and exaggerate our successes. This is done by many people at times when, to those who understand personal value differently, there is absolutely no need for them to discuss their activities at all, let alone to lie about them. A husband and father in our society is too frequently put in a situation in which he feels compelled to succeed or at least appear to succeed. His wife feels it her duty to support him and make him look good. He struggles up the ladder of success at all costs to himself and his family. She climbs behind him, pushing him up with one hand and dragging the children up behind her with the other.

It may appear that I am exaggerating both the extent to which North Americans identify personal value with success and the extent to which we are locked into the work mode of presence. We can certainly get some indication regarding the latter by examining the way we use the word "work." We use it unreflectively to cover nearly everything we do and to describe a great variety of situations that have little, if anything, in common. We work out or work up a sweat. We work on each other's emotions or sympathies. We work at being honest, loving, generous. We work off a debt or work a pump or piece of metal. We work our way through an art gallery or a display and in or out of a sticky situation. This widespread use of the word appears normal to us. Nevertheless, it has the effect of dulling our sensitivity to the variety of our experiences and closes off whole areas of experience to our awareness. When everything is reduced to work, we even lose sight of the value of our work itself.[20]

Because we are so locked into the work mode of being present to one another, we have lost the meaning and value of leisure in our lives. Many people feel guilty if they are not doing something productive. We do not even define leisure in terms of its own inherent meaning and value, but negatively and in terms of work. We say that leisure is time off from work, and we set aside Labour Day each year as a holiday to celebrate work. Haven't we got the cart before the horse? We have less free time now that we work fewer hours a week than we had in the past, yet we remain a people overly concerned with productivity. An economy bent on increasing production must also increase consumption proportionately. Therefore, multimillion dollar industries have arisen to produce the athletic and recreation equipment we need to kill our free time. After all, we can always work at im-

proving our golf, our scuba diving, our tennis,
bridge and solitaire.

The great popularity of that recent genre of literature, the "how to" paperback, is also an indication
of the extent to which we North Americans feel compelled to use leisure time productively. Hobbies can
become like second jobs that provide a second source
of income. Even the world of intimacy and sexual
love has been permeated by the illustrated "how to"
paperback. Making love is reduced to a form of work,
the goal of which is bigger, better and more frequent
orgasms. The fact that this makes the partners very
self-conscious, insecure, turned in on themselves and
overly aware of their performance, to the point that
it destroys the love, seems to go unnoticed.

The more we see ourselves primarily as shapers or
doers, the more closed we become to religious experience. This mode of experience cannot be reduced to
activity. Religion is a response to God and neighbour, but one that essentially starts and ends in
receptivity and openness. It requires the capacity
to allow ourselves to be acted upon, to receive. As
we lose this capacity, we reduce religion to a form
of work. We think about God. We discuss and study
religion and religious problems. We work at doing
good and solving social problems in the name of religion. These are activities of people as workers, not
as religious. Religion necessarily involves the
whole person in a lived response to God and neighbour.
It is a response that encompasses work, leisure,
prayer and all our other experiences as well. It is
the depth dimension of all facets of life, and cannot
be reduced to a series of actions we perform or to a
limited mode of presence like that of work.[21]

The extent to which we identify personal value
with success can also be seen in terms of our drive
to find a meaningful, prestigious job. Too frequently our self-esteem is low, but we feel all will be
well if we can only find the right job. We think our
value comes from the work we do, in spite of the fact
that the opposite is, in fact, the truth. The value
of the work I do depends upon the personal values I
bring to it as a worker. Our failure to understand
that the value of what we do depends on who and what
we are as persons also leads to another serious blind-
ness. We cannot appreciate the uniqueness of the
work we do, because we cannot appreciate our own

uniqueness. We do not recognize the personal quality
of our work that makes it a unique, creative contribution that cannot be duplicated by anyone else.[22]

The over-emphasis we place on work and the personal value we attribute to ourselves, because of it,
keeps us from loving, appreciating and accepting ourselves as we really are. These attitudes cripple us
and make it extremely difficult for us to be personally present to each other in the fullest sense, even
apart from work. Loneliness, personal identity, love
and communication are serious problems for massive
numbers of people in our society. In one form or
other, are these not the problems and the painful
cries of slaves, rather than of free people?

Are citizens really free, if they are locked into
a dominant work mode of presence that permeates their
whole lives? When people cannot recognize their own
personal value and dignity apart from their utility,
has not slavery simply taken a modern, covert and
much more universal form than in the past, in spite
of the fact that it has been legally abolished? The
answer appears to be "yes." Slavery has many modern
forms. This is but one of them. It is allowed to
flourish, and even institutionalized, because it is
politically and economically advantageous. To overcome it and to heal the wounds it is inflicting on
people in every strata of our society requires radical changes in the way we are present to each other
in most facets of our lives. To date, we are unwilling to suffer through the rethinking and restruc-
turing of many fundamental aspects of our lives that
have to be changed, if we are to respect and treat
each other as people. However, without these changes,
we can expect our lives to become more and more impersonal and even dehumanizing. We can also anticipate
an increase in dishonesty, lack of truthfulness and
many other violent forms of crime, as employment becomes more scarce and more competitive and as impersonality gains further inroads in our schools, our
places of employment and even our homes.

Notes

1. Macmurray, pp. 28-29, 39.
2. Ibid., p. 28.
3. Ibid., pp. 29-31.

4.   Ibid., p. 38.
5.   Abraham H. Maslow, *Toward a Psychology of Being*, 2nd. ed. (Princeton, New Jersey: D. Van Nostrand Co., 1968), pp. 86-90.
6.   Ibid., pp. 90-91.
7.   Macmurray, pp. 169-70.
8.   Maslow, pp. 87-88, 184.
9.   Macmurray, pp. 34-35
10. Ibid., pp. 43, 186.
11. Ibid., pp. 186-87.
12. Martin C. Helldorfer, "Work: An Invitation to Growth and Self-Confrontation," *Humanitas*, Vol. VII, No. 2, Fall 1971, pp. 195-96; Martin C. Helldorfer, "The Value of My Work as a Religious," *Sisters Today*, August-September 1973, p. 2; Martin C. Helldorfer, *The Work Trap: Solving the Riddle of Work and Leisure* (Winona, Minnesota: St. Mary's Press, 1981), p. 16.
13. Helldorfer, "Work: An Invitation to Growth and Self-Confrontation," pp.   196-98; Helldorfer, *The Work Trap*, p. 16.
14. Helldorfer, "Work: An Invitation to Growth and Self-Confrontation", pp. 196-97, 199-200.
15. Ibid., pp. 199, 202.
16. Helldorfer, "The Value of My Work as a Religious," p. 3.
17. Helldorfer, "Work: An Invitation to Growth and Self-Confrontation," pp. 200-01.
18. Helldorfer, "The Value of My Work as a Religious," pp. 3-5; Helldorfer, *The Work Trap*, 15, 17-23.
19. Helldorfer, "The Value of My Work as a Religious", p. 6.
20. Ibid., pp. 5-6.
21. Ibid., p. 7.
22. Ibid., pp. 6-7.

PART THREE

OVERCOMING OBSTACLES TO PRESENCE, HONESTY AND TRUTHFULNESS

Chapter 4

OVERCOMING PRESENT INADEQUACIES

Inadequate Concepts of Person

In the preceding chapters, we looked at the meaning of presence, honesty and truth and examined the most common ways by which we are present to each other. In this chapter, we shall attempt to tie together and build upon many of the themes set forth above, by focusing on at least some of the concepts, attitudes and situations in our society that militate against authentic personal presence, and, therefore, also against honesty and truthfulness. We shall begin by zeroing in on some of the inadequacies of two images or models of person that are very influential in our society and on inadequate understandings of the knowledge associated with them.

Concepts or models that express what we think it means to be a person are constantly being developed in all cultures. Three popular examples of such models operative in our society today are the rational animal model, the worker or functionary model and the responder model. We have already discussed the image of person as a relational being or responder at the very outset of this work. Our discussions of functional presence and the work mode of presence have also enabled us to say a great deal about the consequences of understanding ourselves primarily as functionaries or workers. At this point, we shall explore what most people mean today, when they think of people as rational beings or rational animals; and then we shall develop, still further, some of the limitations of the functional model of person. Today, both these images are linked with a particular understanding of knowledge that seriously limits genuine presence and influences our understanding of how we arrive at and live the truth.

Before we go further, I must make it clear that
models of person do not develop in society in isolation from each other, nor are they understood or used
in a mutually exclusive fashion. They overlap and
are very dependent upon each other. For instance,
the functionary acts as an intelligent being in relation to other people. Thus the worker or functionary
model implies and incorporates within itself aspects
of both the rational animal and relational being models. However, when people are seen primarily as functionaries, the personal qualities emphasized by these
other two models are pushed to the background, and
what it means to be a person is summed up in terms of
those qualities that enable us to be good workers or
functionaries. So too, when we conceive of ourselves
primarily as relational beings, we do not deny that
we are agents or workers who act in a virtuous and
rational manner. The rational animal is also understood to be a worker acting in relation with other
people. In all these instances, however, when what
it is to be a person is understood primarily in the
light of one model, the characteristics of the other
models remain eclipsed and effects on personal presence are inevitable.

People constantly use a number of images that
reveal to them what it is to be a person. As we have
just seen, these images are genuinely interdependent
and not intended to be mutually exclusive. Nevertheless, one or other of these images dominates the consciousness of individuals and groups or communities
within our society at any particular time. This is
of genuine concern to us, because the models we emphasize and the way we use them have far-reaching consequences regarding the way we understand and develop
ourselves. For instance, when a particular model
dominates or is very popular in a society for an extended period, it fosters the development of specific,
personal qualities, in the people. These qualities,
in turn, cultivate specific, areas of personal growth
and interest and promote particular institutions compatible with this growth and interest. Other personal qualities and institutions, necessary for growth
in areas of life not given high priority by that model, are not promoted. In fact, their development is
frequently deterred. As we discuss each of the images individually, we shall see specific examples of
this. For the moment, it is sufficient to point out

that some images are advantageous in terms of fostering the qualities essential for genuine personal
presence, honesty and truthfulness, while others are
less effective in this regard.

With these facts in mind, let us move to the rational animal model and the understanding of knowledge associated with it today. This image has had a
long, distinguished tradition in Western civilization.
It has given good service; yet, like all images, it
is partial and limited. Our sole concern is to gain
insight into the degree to which it either promotes
or hinders personal presence as it functions today.
Thus, our discussion will not do justice to this model as it has been understood and functioned throughout the centuries. We shall treat it only as it is
conceived in the popular consciousness of North
Americans now.

For people today, the term rational means something much different from what it meant for the Greeks
and medievalists. Today rational does not ordinarily
include the receptive, contemplative vision which
promotes the kind of intimate, loving knowledge that
fosters personal presence. Both Greek and medieval
scholars distinguished between the power of discursive thought and intuition or simple vision.[1] The
former is the logical, analytical examination of reality that penetrates, abstracts and draws rational
conclusions. The latter is contemplative vision,
which is effortless and receptive rather than analyt-
ic. Aquinas defined contemplation as the "simple,
unimpeded gaze on Truth." It is a long, loving look
at the real, in which the knower, although mentally
alert and active, is open and receptive. The contemplative stance is receptive in that it allows the
truth, beauty and goodness of that which is observed
to reveal and impress themselves on the knower in
their integrity.

The medievalist regarded discursive reasoning as
the central element in human knowledge, but acknowledged that it is accompanied and enriched by the receptive, effortless vision of contemplation. To the
extent that people were understood to participate in
this simple, contemplative vision in a limited way,
they were thought to apprehend the spiritual in the
same way the eye apprehends light and the ear sound,
that is, as whole. Modern philosophers, however,
tend to reduce knowledge to discursive thought alone.

For them, knowledge is achieved, almost exclusively, through such operations as examining, comparing, weighing, measuring, abstracting and deducing, all of which are active, intellectual operations. They leave almost no place for the receptive, contemplative vision that complements and enriches discursive thought. For people today, influenced as we are by modern philosophy and the scientific approach to reality, knowledge is achieved by work; and the amount of effort put into the process of acquiring it is seen as assurance of the truth of the knowledge acquired.

It is not surprising that the rational animal model connotes discursive thought alone for most of us today, given the fact that many modern philosophers reject contemplative vision and maintain that knowledge is exclusively discursive reasoning. With the exception of some scholars, we do not ordinarily associate the receptive, loving knowledge characteristic of contemplative vision with the rational animal model. This drastically reduces its effectiveness as an image of person directed at promoting confidence in the loving, intuitive knowledge that is at the core of personal presence in its fullest sense. Non-discursive knowledge is the most integral and deepest knowledge we can attain of each other. Nevertheless, today, we mistrust it. We place our trust in only the limited facts about each other which we can obtain through such processes as observation, comparison, abstraction and analytical measurements. This limited form of knowledge promotes relationships that are more impersonal, functional and judgmental than personal, receptive and intimate. Therefore, from the perspective of knowledge, the present limitations of the rational animal model are probably most pronounced in the area of fostering such relational qualities as receptivity, sensitivity, affectivity and openness to others as they are in themselves. These are all qualities essential to personal presence in its fullest sense.

As understood by the popular consciousness today, the rational animal model is also very abstract. Too frequently it leaves us with the impression that the human person is constituted and can be understood in terms of its essence alone, and with the illusion that personhood can be known apart from or antecedent to the concrete interactions into which we enter. It is almost as if a person could exist independently of other people, and then later choose to enter into

relationships with them. Relations are seen as somewhat less than primary.

We have already seen, however, that entering into
relations with others is not secondary to the act by
which we come into existence. To exist is to interact, to be related. To come into existence means to
come directly and immediately into relationship with
others. Although having to enter into relations with
others may imply incompleteness, and therefore dependence on that which is external to us, incompleteness
and dependence need not be understood purely and simply as imperfections. Surely these qualities are at
the very basis of our social nature. Being related
to others is so fundamental to our personalities that
we cannot either be or know ourselves apart from our
relations with nature, our neighbour and God.

We have seen that to be a person is to be relational or social to the core. Our relationality, and
the dependence and incompleteness it entails, are
conditions within our nature which orient us outside
of ourselves toward union with others. They are an
internal dynamic, which constitutes us in such a way
that we achieve our perfection and fulfillment in
mutual interaction with each other, not in isolation.
The rational animal model, as understood today, does
not take into account sufficiently the fact that we
simply cannot be people without personal contact with
each other. Relations, and the dependence and incompleteness associated with them, are a very essential
part of what it is to be human. Any model of person
that hopes to promote personal growth and presence
today must make the relational aspect of person central. It must also foster the kind of loving knowledge characteristic of contemplative vision, so that
we shall strive to see each other as unique wholes,
rather than attributing value to each other solely in
terms of individual, functional abilities or skills.

No one word is adequate to sum up the image of
person as worker, but a number of titles are used in
our society to express it. Among them are doer, ac-
tor, agent, functionary and achiever. The focus of
each of these is limited, as is the model of worker
itself. Many facets of person do not come to the
fore and are not emphasized by this model. Yet it is
a very popular model used to convey an understanding
of person that is central to our contemporary
identity.

The image of person as worker or achiever has taken on a more central position in the modern consciousness as large numbers of people have adopted a functional or practical atheism. In cultures characterized by theistic belief, people understood themselves as co-creators who shared responsibility with God for the future of the world. Their lives had meaning, because God gave them meaning and purpose. However, for all practical purposes today, God simply does not enter into the daily lives and experiences of millions of people. Man-come-of-age tends to deny a relationship with a creative, transcendent God. Those who conceive of themselves primarily as doers no longer see themselves as co-creators, but as the sole builders of the future. People alone make history. That is to say, they have total freedom and total responsibility for the future of the world. Their meaning is no longer given to them by God; now they must work to create it for themselves.

In this milieu, scientific knowledge and technical reason are next to absolutized. Symbol, myth, religious knowing and contemplative vision are of diminished value. These traditional methods of arriving at wisdom have been lost and with them ways of thinking about ultimate questions. When the emphasis went off searching to find ultimate values and ends, it shifted to a search for and justification of means and of our very persons. This, in turn, placed even more emphasis on clarity and precision as essential requirements of authentic knowledge. Thus, our concern today centers on the rational, analytical knowledge characteristic of the way we know a fact, not a friend. That personal knowledge, expressed indirectly and symbolically, and most frequently grasped in moments of contemplative vision, is granted minimal validity. However, as we have already seen, an exclusively rational approach to knowledge hinders the receptivity, subjectivity and openness so necessary for obtaining the personal, loving knowledge essential to personal presence, honesty and truthfulness.

Factual knowledge of things and people gives power to the knower over the known and enables a higher degree of control than would otherwise be possible. Possessing power and control over another is a limited good essential to contractual relationships. However, personal presence increases when people form community, rather than when they merely enter into association with each other on functional grounds.

If power and control come to the fore in personal
relationships, they are bound to be destructive, because they frequently lead to contempt, fear and hostility. Once again, therefore, it is evident that
the exclusive respect given to rational knowledge, by
those who have cast themselves into the role of doers
or functionaries, will serve them much better in contractual, more impersonal work situations than in
personal relationships. In fact, it is frequently
destructive of genuine presence.

It is extremely common today to define ourselves
in terms of what we do. When we introduce friends,
we automatically state their occupations after their
names. This is a subtle way of indicating their dignity and value. If a friend is temporarily unemployed, we certainly don't mention it. This practice is
an unconscious expression of a very destructive shift
that has taken place in our society from acknowledging the value of people as such to recognizing their
value in terms of their occupations. The onus is on
each of us to become human. We have to create our
own meaning, dignity and value; and ultimately, the
primary reality each of us must create is her/his own
self.

People, of course, cannot create themselves once
and for all, so many feel constantly driven to produce and to succeed. They are reduced to workers who
are compulsively active, tense and alienated from
themselves, because they must remain far more success
and future oriented than is psychologically healthy
or advantageous to the personal presence required for
genuine friendships and marriage relationships. Excessive competition, dishonesty and lying are only
three of the unfavourable consequences of this understanding of self. Even more detrimental to personal
presence is the inability of achievers to be really
present to others, because they need to be one step
removed, examining the past interaction or planning
the next step, if they are to maintain control and
achieve success.

Too often workers do not feel free to fail, because their whole value as persons is at stake. Since
they can never create total meaning and purpose for
their lives, the temptation is to lose sight of the
creative, ennobling aspects of their work and their
very selves. Those whose self-image is reduced to
that of an agent tend to conceive of themselves as

economic commodities, hands, mere means in a massive
system over which they have little control. A spiritual schizophrenia results in which they see themselves as omnipotent creators making history at one
moment and as impotent functionaries at the next.
Neither the exaggerated image of self as creator
(which is accompanied by an insupportable amount of
responsibility) nor the drastically reduced image of
self as mere means (which destroys a healthy love of
self) promotes an emotionally balanced person capable
of the give and take involved in intimate personal
relationships.

We have already seen that workers need power to
complete their tasks. They have the right to appropriate materials for their own purposes and inevitably
receive personal satisfaction when they achieve success. These factors make the worker the center of
the world of work. However, once a worker steps outside the work world, the same factors and personal
attitudes that brought success at work can become
self-defeating. In interpersonal relationships, reality rarely centers on either person exclusively.
Appropriation, power and control need to give way in
personal relationships to letting the other person
be, to willingness to be weak and overcome, and often
to being a receiver before becoming a giver. When a
person's self-knowledge, identity and self-respect
center on success and satisfaction achieved at work,
the more dominant, aggressive qualities characteristic
of the work mode of presence naturally flow over into
her/his personal relationships and threaten personal
presence. The danger of this threat in any particular
relationship is doubled, of course, when both parties
tend to conceive of themselves primarily as successful
workers.

Fortunately, in many work situations, the characteristics of the work mode of presence are complemented and balanced by the more receptive, caring
attitudes that characterize personal relationships.
Workers relate and respond to each other as real people. Nevertheless, the danger today of conceiving of
ourselves primarily as functionaries is great, because society tends to respect only success and whatever promotes it. Qualities that do not produce success are not valued highly, and we experience our own
personal value less and less apart from what we do.
In this milieu, the intrinsic value of our own persons, the wonder of our personalities and a deep love

of our very selves are constantly eroded. Because we
often lack a sense of our own intrinsic meaning and
dignity, we strive for more meaningful, prestigious
jobs. Having lost sight of our own unique value, we
do not think of ourselves as God's unique gift to
others nor see our work as having a special value
because we performed it. Internal values give us
dignity, not what we do. Functionaries err by reversing this truth, and so are ultimately unable to pre-
serve what is authentically human either in themselves, in their intimate relationships or in society
as a whole.

The image of person as worker tends to be so mas-
culine in its emphasis on aggressivity, control and
power, that it makes it difficult to appreciate the
more feminine qualities of receptivity and openness
that enable both women and men to be genuinely present to others. Some psychologists in the Jungian
tradition recognize the *animus* as that focused
awareness that is so essential to science and the development of technology. They indicate that it frequently functions to the detriment of the *anima*, which
they characterize as a more diffused awareness or
ability to be present at a more extensive level.
They indicate that without a balance of the two, a
person's ability to achieve communion with others by
loving and receiving love is limited. In fact, over-
emphasis on the achiever model, which is so widespread
today, tends to restrict many people's activities to
work experience. Work becomes the central factor in
maintaining their identity and using their time, even
when it is not necessary economically.

People who are locked into the work mode of presence ordinarily perceive with only their own needs
and interests in mind. As a result, the intrinsic
nature of the things and people they observe is frequently not seen at all. Only one side of the polar-
ities or contradictions in that which they observe
comes to the fore. The whole is not grasped because
only individual aspects of whole people or things can
be abstracted and compared on a continuum. The knowledge acquired by such observers is partial; it contains individual truths about people and things, but
not the truth of these people or things as such.
Although these observers may not realize how limited
their knowledge of others is, those known are usually
aware that they are known only as means, and not as
ends, with value in and for themselves. Resentment

and fear frequently result, because people are willing
to serve and to be useful to others, but they dislike
being seen as useful objects, and simply abhor being
used.

We are more than functionaries, doers or
achievers. To be reduced to repeatedly proving our
value is to be required to perform perpetually, and
the strain and tension that accompany such a position
are marks of the personal bankruptcy that results.
Community, without which genuine, personal presence
is simply impossible, is not based on achievement, but
on love and respect for others. When the worker model
of person dominates the popular consciousness, and is
not modified and balanced by other models, it does not
foster this kind of mutual respect, nor does it promote the loving, personal knowledge on which deep
friendships and solid marriages can be grounded.
Herein lie its ultimate inadequacies as a base on
which to build a society characterized by authentic,
personal presence, honesty and truthfulness.

The Need for Loving Knowledge

In our discussions of the work mode of presence
and of presence in its fullest sense, we talked about
different ways by which we come to know each other.
In this chapter we have already focused on the limitations in the knowledge we acquire of each other,
when either the rational animal or the worker model
are allowed to dominate our consciousness. These
discussions leave no doubt that knowledge, truth and
personal presence are intimately related. The process
by which we attempt to acquire knowledge of each other
determines to a great extent whether we really grasp
their truth, and grasping their truth is absolutely
essential to being personally present to them.

Our problem, then, is to try to understand how we
can get to know people in the way that will enable us
to be most fully present to them. Some philosophies
indicate that our intellect grasps the truth of that
which we know first, and then presents this truth to
our will to choose or love. This leaves us with the
impression that the act of our will (loving) is entirely excluded from the process of obtaining an objective knowledge (the truth) of that which we come
to know. Can this be so? Does not our discussion of

personal and impersonal knowledge bring this understanding of the way we grasp the truth and goodness
of people into question? Is it adequate to say that
our intellect grasps the truth of that which we know
first, and then presents it to our will to love? Or,
on the other hand, ought love to be present and active
in the very process of acquiring true knowledge? In
my estimation, inadequacies in approaches to understanding how knowledge and love are related and how
knowledge and truth are acquired are at the core of
many of our present problems regarding personal presence.

Hans Urs von Balthasar presents an understanding
of the relationship between knowledge and love in
acquiring truth that is extremely relevant to our
understanding of personal presence. He starts by
relating the objective and subjective sides of knowing. On the objective side, people naturally order
their perception to the structures of things as they
present themselves to be known. That is to say,
things disclose themselves to be known in their own
truth or reality, and, by this very fact, place limitations or controls on the activity of the knower.
However, on the more subjective side of knowing, there
is relative freedom and selectivity in acquiring
knowledge. That is to say, the process of coming to
know reality also involves freedom and spontaneity.
All of us are open to the whole of reality, yet many
things present themselves that we do not choose to
integrate into our overall vision of the world. This
exclusion is partially due to our limited capacity
for knowledge, but it is also a sign of our freedom
to choose to know only those things that conform to
our own inner structure or to our own world view. In
our commitment to truth, we can choose to overlook
inessential facts and forego knowledge of many things.
This voluntary exclusion of truths we find to be in-
opportune is complemented by a voluntary opennnes to
truths we choose to integrate into our vision. Our
capacity to be selective regarding the truth of things
we choose to know is of ethical significance, of
course, because it is conditioned by our attitude
toward ultimate questions of existence. Evaluation
and choice, therefore, do not occur after we acquire
knowledge, but act as selecting and emphasizing factors in our very acts of knowing.[2]

Things and people constantly reveal their truth
to us, yet they always remain truer and richer than

any of their self-revelations. Everything has a capacity to be for itself; yet at the core of every
being there is also an impetus to disclose itself.
In the last analysis, the tendency within things to
exist or be for themselves and their impulse to participate are one and the same. These tendencies form
the one, indivisible elucidation of being. Thus, the
real meaning of being lies in love, and knowledge is
explicable only through and for love. One person's
willingness to reveal her/himself and another person's willingness to receive that revelation form one
act of mutual submission. Therefore, love and truth
are inseparable. We cannot attain knowledge without
the operation of our will, nor truth without love.
Love is the aspect of truth that guards an ever new
secret and does not permit the person knowing to limit
that which is known to part of what it actually is;
love attends to that which is beyond what is revealed
at any moment.[3]

Because we can only attain truth through love,
only those who love can grasp a proper vision of it.
Only those who love are truly willing to disclose
themselves and to be receptive to the revelations of
those who have opened themselves in love. Love enables us to attain that wherein the truth of each
other's being emerges. Love is the ground of truth,
so that love and truth become inseparable; neither
one is antecedent to the other.[4] A true knower is
a true lover. A person who does not love is incapable of acquiring true knowledge.

People who are capable of acquiring a loving
knowledge of others are really free in their process
of knowing. They approach those who are the object of
their knowledge with a special attentiveness or free
orientation that is best described in terms of genuine
availability. As subjects (knowers), such people possess a perceptive openness and a desire to listen
without interrupting the revelations of those whom
they are striving to know. Their acts of knowing are
at one and the same time acts of loving that prefer
the good and truth of those to whom they are listening
to their own particular good and truth. Those revealing themselves feel at home with such a person,
so they are able to reveal their being and truth in a
manner not possible under other circumstances. In
fact, at times, in the act of knowing, a loving knower
can help those revealing themselves to arrive at a
new, deeper self-knowledge.[5]

Those who attempt to know others, by approaching
them with a loving orientation, achieve a special
vision of those they come to know, a vision that is
both objective and idealizing. Those who are known
are aware ideally of what they might become, but they
cannot achieve their ideal selves without assistance.
In order that their hidden potentialities be actualized, they need others who see these undeveloped
capabilities existing objectively in them. The potentialities under question are there, but are only
visible to a loving knower who believes they can be
realized. We need to be known by others who believe
in and love us. In some instances, the creative vision of a loving knower even discovers possibilities
completely unknown to the person who possesses them.
Herein lies the real mystery of freedom in knowledge;
it is a mystery of love. The ideal image of the
person known is attained by the loving knower. This
image is equally objective and subjective. It is
objective, because it is only through the activity of
the knower that it is actualized or attains actual,
objective truth. It is subjective, because it is not
contrived, but only illucidated, by the knower. The
loving subject knows that the possibilities s/he
sees in people are genuine and regards their realization as the action of those people. Yet those who
are loved are inevitably aware that it was the creative activity of someone else's love that held up
their ideal image to them and gave them the confidence
and courage to dare to realize it.[6]

In truth, the ideal is the possible. The ideal
reality of those who are loved exists, at any moment,
only in the love of those by whom they are loved.
The authentic place for the ideal image of a person
is in the personal love of others, because it is there
that it can bloom. The creation and realization of
this true, ideal image of the person loved is a creative act in which the lover and beloved both try to
shape reality according to the exemplar they envisage.
It is the faith and confidence of a knower, whose·
knowledge of the other is quickened by love, that
enables the person loved to have confidence in the
ideal set forth for her/him. The actualization by
the beloved of this ideal self may be slow or rapid.
Nevertheless, this actualization does not take place
in steps, nor is it to be measured according to the
efforts that are made to achieve it. Such an approach
removes freedom from the knowledge of the lover and
introduces an element of disinterested impartiality

in her/his image of the beloved. When this occurs,
knowledge is reduced to an impersonal, rather than a
loving knowledge; and so loses its power of reality
and realization. When the knowledge of the knower is
reduced to a mere image of genuine knowledge, the
beloved is left in isolation with the overpowering
task of trying to imitate that mere image from day to
day.

    In reality, the process of realizing our true
selves is far from an isolated pursuit. A loving
knower conceives and maintains the ideal image of
those s/he loves as their true reality, and in all
their interactions behaves as though they already
correspond with this image. This does not imply that
the knower is either blind to or deceived about the
unfulfilled reality of those loved, about the distance
between the real and the ideal in their lives. A
loving knower is not interested in the faults of those
loved; by overlooking faults and imperfections s/he
simply allows the present, incomplete image of those
loved to sink into nothingness. In the eyes of a
loving knower incomplete images of those loved have
no worth, no consistency and no right to exist. These
images are treated by love as having no claims on
existence. Since they are denied the right to express themselves as the truth of those loved, by not
being allowed to disclose themselves, over time, they
are destroyed or annihilated. That is to say, the
creative revelation of the true or ideal images of
the people loved brings about the creative destruction
of their real, incomplete images of themselves.[7]

    In order to harmonize themselves with the creative
process of becoming discussed above, those who are
loved act as if their ideal were already real. Most
certainly, at times, they will fail and be inconsistent in this pursuit. Nevertheless, they abuse truth
if they concentrate on their failures. People who
experience the love of others are aware that those
who love them have an objective knowledge of their
real, imperfect selves; but they also know that those
who love them reject their incomplete images, in order
to know the reality of their ideal selves as their
truth. This loving support enables them to find the
internal strength to transform themselves. It is the
power of affirmation, therefore, in loving knowledge
that enables those who are loved to become their true
selves.

Truth reveals, but also knows when to conceal.
Most of us are conscious of the fact that we cannot
transform ourselves simply by being made aware of our
faults. Nor are we capable of experiencing sorrow for
our failures, simply because they are revealed to us.
The fact is that we can only experience sorrow for our
inconsistencies and failures when we see them in view
of our ideal or most authentic selves. When we know
that our ideal selves are anticipated by those who
love us as our authentic truth, we can muster up the
courage to strive to attain this truth, even when it
appears unattainable. At times, when we fall back
into the old mistakes that dominated our incomplete
image of ourselves, we simply have to trust (know)
that we are temporarily living a fact that is already
overcome, and therefore no longer actually real.[8]

As we come to appreciate the transforming power
of loving knowledge, we gain deeper insight into the
awesome responsibility placed on our shoulders by our
knowledge of each other. We are not only responsible
to know what other people are at the moment, but also
what they ought to be (what their ideal images are).
Our knowledge of others cannot help but act as a guide
by which they become themselves. The danger of presenting false ideals and purely subjective images,
that might deceive those we know, is very great.
Only God's knowledge of them is their exemplar and
the measure and test of their truth. He alone possesses the idea (ideal) of things in himself. Thus,
if our knowledge is not to be deceptive, it must look
to the image of things known by God. We can only
know people, as they ought to be, when we see them in
God. By striving to know others in reference to God,
we arrive at their true image and can justifiably
encourage them to pursue that image of themselves.
On the other hand, without reference to God, our
highest acts of loving knowledge, those by which we
share in the very co-operative realization of the
truth of each other, are simply Promethian efforts
without justification. We certainly need an abundance
of grace to love and know each other in relation to
God in whom the image of knowledge and love of all
things fully coincide.[9]

In an engraced context, in which we can strive to
know reality and freely assess situations as God sees
them, we become involved in the very formation of the
truth of reality itself. In revealing ourselves in
truth and receiving the free revelations of others,

we fulfill ourselves as spiritual beings and achieve
our happiness. However, to the extent that we fail
to participate in witnessing to and receiving truth,
we destroy ourselves as spiritual beings. Because
both the expression and application of truth involve
freedom, prudence (practical wisdom) is our most basic
norm in revealing and receiving truth. However, our
practical wisdom, in turn, must be directed by the
higher guiding principle of love. Love is both the
disinterested communication of our own, unique being
and the disinterested acceptance of others. Mutual
self-revelation is truthful and insightful only when
it is accompanied by mutual reverence and dedication
of people to each other.[10]

Where love is not present, we can attain particular truths correctly, but our understanding is com-
parable to the vision of a short-sighted person--our
view of details is sharp, but we fail to obtain a
vision of the whole. The stance of a person toward
someone s/he does not love is most accurately described as a cold objectivity, an impressive silence,
in which the words of the person to be known resound
without protection. Such a non-loving knower takes
the position of an impartial judge in whom there is
no real movement of knowledge toward the person to be
known. Since the person known can only fulfill her/
himself in the sphere of subjectivity (in and through
the knowledge of a loving knower), her/his fulfillment
is deterred because self-disclosure is made very
difficult.

Where the motive for self-revelation is egoism or
personal advantage, once again, individual truths are
grasped as material propositions, but not as genuine
truth. Knowing carried out for personal advantage is
in conflict with truth that is motivated by love.
Those who share truth, in order to profit by it, may
appear to give of themselves to others, but they are
really presenting an appearance of openness in order
to conceal themselves. The contradiction in action
that occurs here places them outside the truth, and
makes the revelation that takes place more deceptive
than true. Apart from loving knowledge, imitations
of truth possess elements of truth in only a formal
way, but these fall short of truth, because they are
not genuine self-revelations. In fact, such formally
correct statements do not serve truth, and through
their limited truth frequently help to promulgate
error.[11]

This entire discussion of the place and activity
of love in the process of obtaining a true knowledge
of people ties together on a deeper level many themes
concerning personal presence introduced in earlier
chapters. We saw at the very outset that people are
present to each other when they play a role in each
other's process of becoming. We have seen throughout
most of our previous discussions that love and personal knowledge are essential for creating that immediate (unmediated), personal presence that alone is
fulfilling, creative and abiding. Now we see that
loving knowledge, above all else, is that which enables us to enter into each other's lives and play a
role in each other's personal transformation and
growth.

The added insight gained by examining the role of
love in the process of acquiring personal knowledge
enables us to affirm emphatically that personal presence in the fullest sense is simply impossible in the
absence of mutual, loving knowledge. Thus, we see why
the impersonal, factual knowledge we prize so highly
is limited and incomplete (lacking in truth). It simply cannot create the genuine, personal presence we
need to become our ideal selves, because it lacks the
power of affirmation that accompanies loving knowledge. In brief, we see just how big a mistake we are
making when we put more confidence in impersonal,
objective knowledge than in the personal knowledge we
acquire through the give and take that occur in
friendships and love relationships.

From a slightly different perspective, our present
discussion enables us to see that there are poten-
tially disastrous consequences for our personal self-
realization and for the development of a milieu that
can support family life, when we constantly subordinate loving knowledge and personal relationships to
the impersonal, functional aspects of living. In all
honesty, we must also ask if it is possible to develop
the kind and level of community that are required to
maintain a high level of civilization, when we conceive of and reduce ourselves primarily to workers.
Too many of our most personal qualities are simply
not realized in a context in which the ideal self we
see and call forth in each other is reduced to that
of an efficient worker.

If the obstacles to personal presence and the
problems associated with dishonesty and lack of truth-

fulness in our society are to be overcome, we need to give much higher priority to the relational image of person and must respect the kind of loving knowledge of each other that will enable us to realize our ideal or true selves. Personal existence is co-existence, in which more emphasis must be placed on presence and sharing than on competing. Human experience is shared experience and human life, a common life. In attempting to know and be present to each other, we have to shift the emphasis off rational analysis, domination and utility, in order to focus on listening, sensitivity and adaptability. Allowing ourselves to be open to and acted upon by others will take on a significance not recognized when the rational and functional are allowed to dominate. We are subjects whose personalities and creativity cannot blossom without mutual, loving self-revelation. When we make the relational aspect the starting point for understanding what it is to be human, emphasis will fall more directly on intersubjectivity, communication, sharing and the loving knowledge that makes these other activities possible. Together they form the foundation for genuine, personal presence.

Notes

1. The analysis of the relationship between discursive and contemplative thought that follows relies heavily on Josef Pieper's, *Leisure: The Basis of Culture*, trans. by Alexander Dru (New York: The New American Library, Inc., A Mentor Book, 1963), pp. 25-29.
2. Hans Urs von Balthasar, "The Freedom of the Subject," *Cross Currents*, Vol. 12, No. 1, Winter 1962, pp. 13-14.
3. Ibid., pp. 15-16.
4. Ibid., p. 16.
5. Ibid., pp. 16-17.
6. Ibid., p. 18.
7. Ibid., p. 19.
8. Ibid., pp. 19-21.
9. Ibid., pp. 21-22.
10. Ibid., pp. 22-24.
11. Ibid., pp. 16-17, 24-25.

Chapter 5

REDUCING PRESENT OBSTACLES

Reducing Fear and Hatred as Unconscious Motivations

Our discussion of fear and hatred, as unconscious motivations for action, brings us back, once again, to the thought of John Macmurray. What follows is both consistent with and parallel to what we have already said about personal and impersonal relations, attitudes and knowledge. It also has the advantage of viewing fear, hatred and love as unconscious motivations within the much larger context in which personal development is seen as a natural extension of a child's original motivation pattern in relation to its mother. Thus, this discussion will help us to touch base once again with our point of departure in understanding ourselves as relational beings. It will also enable us to examine these three unconscious motives for action in relation to the conscious motives and intentions that are operative as well in moving us to act.

We saw at the outset of this work that the original motivation pattern of a child's behaviour in relation to its mother is the starting point for all its subsequent development. This pattern has both a positive and negative pole, each of which is implicitly referred outside the child, first to its mother and later to other people as well. This original pattern remains as the basic pattern of personal motivation throughout the child's development. Normally, this development takes the child from total dependence on its parents to a healthy, mutual interdependence among people who are seen as equals. The goal of this process, therefore, is not independence; but a relatively impersonal, indirect dependence on society. The underlying motivation pattern that re-

mains constant throughout the child's life is that
universal motive in all of us to communicate with
others. In fact, this orientation toward communication is common to all our experience, and even determines its form.[1]

Since our actions are defined by our intentions,
knowledge is present in our action as that which determines our purposeful activities. However, organic
impulses, that is, actions that are simply a reaction
to stimuli, without knowledge, are also common in our
behaviour. Thus, as in our discussion of impersonal
and personal relations, we must acknowledge that the
positive presupposes its own negative--a motive consciousness that can determine purposeful activity
without knowledge, simply as a reaction to a stimulus.
We see, therefore, that our intentions presuppose our
motivation, so that a complete account of our actions
must consider both our motivation and our
intentions.[2]

When we distinguish between the motives and intentions for our behaviour, we find that our motives
are relatively few, but extraordinarily persistent.
Nevertheless, the behaviour they bring about is very
diversified and complex, because motives are influenced by knowledge and behaviour is determined, at
least to some extent, by the situations in which we
find ourselves having to act. Normally we focus our
attention on the intentions we have for acting, so
that we are ordinarily unconscious of our motives.
In fact, it is only when a particular action we want
to perform is inhibited, so that we cannot express
the motive behind it overtly, that the motive rises
to the level of our consciousness and expresses itself
in an emotion that frequently disturbs our consciousness and our normal way of acting.[3]

At this point, we shall identify the positive and
negative poles of our personal motivation as love and
fear. In doing so, we are not referring to them as
emotions that rise to our consciousness and disturb
us, nor are we speaking of them simply as organic
impulses associated with sexual passion or panic terror. When understood as original motives of action,
love and fear are thought of in the far broader sense
in which they function as unconscious motives of behaviour that determine the direction in which we expend our energy. As original motives of personal action, they are distinguished by their reference to

someone other than ourselves. They are personal motives for action, because they move us to express our
need to communicate with each other, a need that can
only be satisfied by the responses we receive from
others. Thus, since the behaviour love and fear motivate needs to be complemented by the responses of
others, it is incomplete in itself. This, of course,
leaves us vulnerable.[4] It is in this context of
vulnerability that we shall press even further to
understand love, fear and hatred as unconscious motives of action, not as conscious emotions.

In positive and negative motivation, our reference to other people differs. In the case of positive
motivation (love), our reference is direct; love is
love for someone else. In the case of negative motivation (fear), our reference if indirect. Fear is
fear for myself, but at the same time it is fear of
someone else. Fear for myself refers to the behaviour of some other person or persons. Because we
need others in order to become ourselves, our primary
fear is that others will not respond to our communication (expression of need), and as a consequence, our
personal existence will be frustrated or threatened.
From this analysis, we see very clearly that love and
fear, as personal motives, fall within the realm of
personal relations. They are the positive and negative poles of the our single motivation to communicate. Love is the positive pole, and fear, the negative, that presupposes love and is subordinate to
it. They are operative in all our action--the positive containing, being constituted by and subordi-
nating its own negative.[5]

We shall propose reasons indicating why this relationship has to be so by re-examining themes that
have already been set forth. Action contains movement
and knowledge. Whereas action is deliberative, reaction to a stimulus is impulsive. Thus our motivation
to act must contain an inhibiting element, one that
will prevent us from making an immediate, habitual
response, yet move us to reflect and decide what to
do in the light of our specific situation. By its
very nature, fear inhibits. Even our most positive
acts must contain an element of negative motivation,
if they are not to be reckless. For instance, in all
our actions there is an awareness of the possibility
of error. In the normal situations in which we interact, negative motivation is present, because the fulfillment of one person's action depends on her/his

own intention and motivation and on the responses of others. Thus, our success as agents, always depends to some extent on the intentions and motivations of other people. Since they may not make the responses we desire and need, none of our actions are entirely without the negative motivation of fear. Nevertheless, no action can be entirely motivated by fear. Total, negative motivation would paralyze us as agents or doers. Some positive motivation is required, if we are to produce any form of deliberate action.[6]

In all actions that are positively motivated, love dominates and subordinates fear to itself. In those actions that are negatively motivated, fear dominates and love is subordinated to it. In either case, the subordinated pole has a discriminating function. Negatively motivated action is defensive; the agent is the center of reference for the act (fear is for oneself). Positively motivated action has as its center people other than the agent (love is for the other).[7]

Recognizing whether an action is self or other centered is of prime importance in understanding the way we subordinate our motive for it to our intention. Let us illustrate this by the example of a mother's action for her child. A mother's positive motivation includes a negative element within itself. In a situation in which her child is in danger, such as a fire, a mother's action is accompanied by fear, anxiety or even terror. Yet, she is positively, not negatively motivated. Her action is other centered; her fear is for her child's safety, not for her own. In fact, her fear itself is an expression of her deep love for her child. In other words, her fear is a negative, subordinate element in her positive, loving motivation to save her child regardless of danger to herself. Here we see that fear, the emotion that is felt at the moment of the mother's action, is not the motive of her action. Thus we can affirm that emotions are components, but not necessarily defining characters, of our motivation to act.

It is the character of the situations in which we find ourselves that determines the presence of one or other specific emotion in our consciousness. The specific emotion that we feel is not likely to reveal the real motive behind our action in most situations, because, as we have already seen, one of the major conditions for an emotion to rise to the level of

consciousness is its inhibition as a motive of action.
The mother's terror when her child is in danger is
occasioned by the fact that she must act without regard for her own safety. Her fear for herself is
inhibited as a motive for her action. Because it
cannot express itself overtly, it is reflected back
into her consciousness as a strong emotion. The absence of fear in her action explains its intrusive
appearance in her consciousness and also indicates
why it is so difficult for her, and for us, in most
instances, to determine the real motives behind our
actions.[8]

From analyzing the interaction of the positive
and negative motives operative in situations, it is
possible to recognize a third, original motive which
we shall identify as hatred. We can say that this
motive is original, because it is a universal component in people's interactions, and derivative, because
it presupposes love and fear as operative motives.
Its origin is in the frustration of love by fear.
For instance, when a positively motivated act of love
is refused a response, it is frustrated. In fact,
when we refuse to enter into a mutual relation with
someone who has made an offer of friendship to us, in
general, we frustrate that person's personal life
absolutely. The person whose offer of friendship has
been rejected is thrown back on her/his own self and
the negative pole of her/his motivation necessarily
becomes dominant. S/he becomes afraid for her/his
personal existence, and naturally resents the action
of the other. In situations in which continued interaction between two such people cannot be avoided,
this resentment frequently becomes hatred. Hatred
can become a persistent motive in the personal relation of the person rejected; but not, of course, a
persistent emotion of which s/he is conscious. As an
original motive for action, therefore, hatred is one
component of a complex motivation. However, it is
not necessarily dominant and is subject to the control
of intention.[9]

We see, therefore, that rejecting a personal relationship is the negative aspect of personal relatedness and leads to mutual rejection by the parties
involved. When my personal existence is threatened,
all I can do, on the unconscious level of motivation,
is reciprocate by threatening (rejecting) the person
who has rejected me. However, when the motive of
either fear or hatred dominates my relation to an-

other, the negative relation that results remains in
me in the form of a practical contradiction. I maintain, but also refuse, the relationship at the same
time. My positive motive for maintaining it is inhibited by my negative motive, and my very being is frustrated or stultified. If my hatred is not intentionally controlled, it can result in violence. Thus, it
is not suprising that we ordinarily contrast love and
hatred, in spite of the fact that the opposition between them, as we see from what has been said above,
is more complex and more fundamental than this would
imply.10

This theoretical discussion of the relationship
between love, fear and hatred, as underlying motives
for behaviour, provides fertile ground from which we
can glean new insights regarding our built-in obstacles to personal presence, honesty and truthfulness,
especially in the impersonal and functional relations
to which we devote so much of our time and energy.
Nevertheless, there may be those who feel that far
too much emphasis is being placed on negative motiva-
tion--on fear. Thus, before we focus on these insights, it may be well to concentrate for a moment on
a few of the causes of fear in our society in order
to assure ourselves that the attention we have given
to it as a pervasive, unconscious motive behind our
behaviour is not way out of balance.

Psychologists have been telling us for years that
as adults we develop innumerable ways of subtly concealing and denying our fears. In fact, a great deal
of the time we are not even conscious of the fact
that we are afraid. Without knowing it, we are afraid
to get too much knowledge of ourselves. Facts that
might lead us to lose respect for ourselves, by revealing our weaknesses, sins or lack of ability are
simply repressed by a defensive fear that protects
our self-esteem. Nor are we really honest with ourselves in other areas where we avoid facing the truth
about our talents and potential creativity out of
fear of the burdens of responsibility and the dangers
and loneliness that might beset us, if we really develop our creative potential. These examples illustrate instances in which we are motivated by subtle
fears to avoid being genuinely honest and truthful
with ourselves.

We can also look at an even more extensive area
in which we avoid acquiring knowledge and relating it

in social and work situations. Here, fear moves us
to be even more defensive. Those who are dependent
on others for employment, or other necessities, often
find it does not pay to know too much or to express
the truth freely, because their knowledge can be
threatening to those on whom they depend. When children and those most dependent on others for their basic
necessities of life are forced to choose between their
own personal development and maintaining a relationship with someone on whom they depend, too frequently
fear moves them to choose the latter. These defensive
techniques are not exercised by all of us to the same
extent. Those among us who are more self-actualizing
are less likely to be inhibited by fear in this kind
of situation, and so have more opportunity to become
free, mature, truthful and honest.

Recent discoveries regarding the great extent of
space and time have the tendency to make us see ourselves and our actions as small and relatively insig-
nificant. Yet, at the same time, we see ourselves as
making history and as having a responsibility toward
future generations for the condition in which they
will find the universe. When awareness of these realities is combined with the rapid rate of change
today and the massive technological, industrial and
govermental institutions that tend to make so many
facets of our lives impersonal, we can easily become
fearful about our own meaning and for our own survival. We do what we can to cope, but at great expense to our personal lives.

The emphasis we place on maximizing efficiency
today is too frequently at the expense of what is
authentically personal. The inefficiency of ordinary
people has far more widespread and disastrous consequences than it ever did in the past, because of the
extended frontiers of our communication networks and
of our places of employment. We cannot afford to
make mistakes today. The rate of communication and
production is so rapid that there is little time to
correct errors and avoid their unfavourable consequences. Yet, at the same time, it is more difficult
for us to remain competent in our field or to avoid
the danger of having our job done away with by automation. These realities of work life today increase
fear and promote defensive behaviour.

As the need for specialization increases, we become more and more cut off from each other. Theoreti-

cally, specialists complement and support each other.
Yet, in practice, they are frequently a threat to
each other, because they become polarized and each
finds it harder and harder to keep abreast of the
other's specialization. Communication among specialists tends to become more difficult and this causes
anxiety and fear, especially since the value systems
by which many of us lived as we grew up are in a state
of flux, and we have little assurance that we shall
be respected by others in time of crisis. At times,
many people around us are reduced to simply trying to
hang on. The differences between the rich and poor
are increasing visibly, and those with reasonable
means are afraid of losing what they have. All these
factors make the unconscious, negative motivation of
fear very operative in most facets of our lives today.

Having spent a few moments looking at the innumerable causes of fear in our society, let us return to
our discussion of fear and hatred as negative motivations. Although both positive and negative motives
are always present in all our activities, the positive
motive of love normally dominates the negative. This
means that we are ordinarily oriented toward friendship and personal presence. Whenever we freely enter
into mutual self-revelation, honesty and truthfulness
are at their maximum. However, the unconscious, negative motivation of fear and hatred are more operative
in our behaviour than we are ordinarily inclined to
believe. Frequently, we are unaware of our negative
motivation, because fear and hatred can be dominant,
unconscious motives at times when we do not experience
them as emotions on the conscious level. This realization challenges us to take a serious look at all
those functional relationships that characterize our
business and work lives.

We have already seen that functional relations
are of their very nature impersonal, although they
can be open to the personal. This means that love
(willing the good of the other person) is not necessarily present where genuine concern is not at least
striven for among workers and between workers and
administrators. Under such circumstánces, it is not
likely that the unconscious, positive motive of love
will dominate our negative motives of fear and hatred.
Thus fear and hatred can easily come to the fore in
our unconscious motivation at work, regardless of the
fact that we are unaware of it. This very realistic
possibility may well account for much of the dishones-

ty and lack of truthfulness that pervade not only
business and industry, but our whole world of work.

Fear of the world cuts communication with it.
Similarly, fear of others greatly reduces, if it does
not cut off, communication with them. It is essential, therefore, to look seriously at how we see ourselves and how others see us, that is to say, at who
and what we are in our own eyes and in the eyes of
others. If I know myself only as I appear to myself,
and not as I appear to others, those actions of mine
that seem to me to be determined by other people's
attitudes and responses to me might well be free acts
on my part. When, in fact, my own motivation is negative, my action is defensive and is determined by my
own tendency to be defensive and to isolate
myself.[11] The impression received by others is
often very different from that which I think I am
projecting. Thus, I may easily instill uneasiness,
or even fear, in others unintentionally. In such
instances, where my conscious motives and intentions
are positive and co-operative, it is very difficult
for me to conceive how others can possibly be threatened by or fearful of me. Yet, this can be the case.
All of these illustrations point to instances of
self-revelation that are meant to promote personal
presence, yet impede it and make being honest and
truthful very difficult.

From analyzing our unconscious motivation, we can
also gain insight into what is operative within us
when we become self-conscious. I know myself in and
through interactions with you. I know you as an object, but I also know you as a subject who, in turn,
also knows me as an object. Especially in functional
relations and situations in which I am dependent on
you, I can readily fear your evaluation of me and my
abilities. Fear of a negative evaluation or hostility
on your part make me become self-conscious. I see
myself as an object being valued negatively by you,
and my inclination to reveal myself is immediately
inhibited. There is a natural tendency in me not to
give myself away, but to keep my truth to myself. On
the one hand, what I reveal may be minimal, but true.
On the other, I may pretend to be or to support what
I do not approve, so that my actions are positively
misleading. In either instance, the degree of personal presence between us is very limited and honest,
truthful communication between us is minimal.

Such a situation assures that my motivation toward you will remain negative. Ironically, this situation undoubtedly also assures my co-operation with you, at least to the point of protecting myself and achieving those ends that are of interest to both of us. My fear, hatred and hostility are restrained, or even suppressed, in situations in which my co-operation is required, and where it can be maintained only by at least some degree of constraint. I may also achieve satisfaction in this situation as the result of accomplishing objectives that are good. In fact, it may even appear to both of us that our interaction is really satisfying and fulfilling our need for each other.[12] This impression must be challenged.

We have already seen that we realize ourselves most fully through knowing, loving and enjoying each other, and that the knowledge that enables us to become our ideal selves is not a merely factual, but a loving knowledge. There is no doubt that strong emotions sharpen our attention and observation and enable us to see facts and acquire knowledge of others that we would not be able to acquire otherwise. Nevertheless, we need only recall that love enables us to obtain a knowledge of others that is more holistic, other than and beyond the factual knowledge we can amass about them by rational analysis alone. Both positive and negative emotions sharpen our focus, but they also direct our attention to different aspects of those we observe.

When positive motivation dominates the way we see another person, our negative emotions are not eliminated. Their action as a restraining, inhibiting factor in our vision enables us to see the person's limitations at the same time as our positive motivation focuses on her/him as a whole. However, when negative motivation dominates, our knowledge of the other is reduced to facts; the ideal vision of that person is simply not seen and the isolated facts that are seen are not grasped in their true context. Therefore, we can say that our knowledge of others is a function of either our love or fear of them. If it is a function of love, it is true; if it is a function of fear, it is very limited and to some extent an illusion. Therefore, we must affirm that negatively motivated interaction does not satisfy the parties' real need to know each other.

In situations where co-operation is required over

a long period of time, the co-operation achieved
through negative motivation does not provide adequate
satisfaction either. There is a deeper need for reconciliation and for genuine care for each other that
remains unsatisfied. The continued, negative motivation inhibits the movement toward deeper personal
presence that is normal where people are present to
each other for lengthy periods. Even if all the ex-
changes between those involved in such a situation
are honest and truthful, we simply cannot say that
their relationship is characterized by either honesty
(in the sense of really being present to themselves
or each other as they really are) or truthfulness (in
the sense of doing or living the truth in love).

Although an action cannot have contradictory intentions, it can have contradictory motives in the
form of suppressed, unconscious motives. These motives can and do find expression in our action so
that, at times, we act in ways that we do not intend.
This ambiguity in motivation also creates tension
within and among us.[13] It is not surprising, therefore, that in work situations, characterized as they
are by impersonality, there is a lack of mutual support, an absence of constructive, co-operative action
that is clearly appropriate, and, at times, even
lapses into destructive behaviour that is seemingly
inexplicable.

In situations where co-operation is really required, yet the motivation of those involved is negative, individuals invariably try to achieve security
by doing whatever they can to defend themselves. In
their fear for themselves, in relation to each other
and in their defense of themselves, against the threat
of each other, both employees and employers can really
develop a mutual anger and even hatred. The co-operation among them may take the form of either submissive or aggressive action. In such circumstances,
either form of action is predominantly self-centered
and defensive. By being submissive to the demands of
someone in authority, an employee may attempt to put
that person under an obligation to protect her/him.
By being aggressive, s/he may attempt to make the
administrator afraid of not providing such protection.
In either case, the negative motivation excludes mutuality, and, therefore, personal presence in any
genuine sense. It also reduces honesty and truthfulness as we have described them, even when there is no
deliberate effort to deceive on the part of anyone

involved.[14]

From what we have said of love, fear and hatred as negative, unconscious motives for action, we can conclude that if the rampant dishonesty and lack of truthfulness in the world of business and work are to be significantly reduced, we must take steps to limit impersonality in the work world. Although the attributes that characterize the work mode of presence will always remain in the foreground in work situations, they must be tempered by more loving knowledge and care for each other. Efforts must be made to make the plant, office or department a place of personal interaction that possesses many of the characteristics of a community, rather than being merely a place of association. However, before we elaborate on this change, we shall focus for a moment on how hostility, prejudice and competition also act as factors reducing presence, honesty and truthfulness in the world of work. They too prevent it from being a locus of community.

Reducing Hostility, Prejudice and Competition

Positive, spiritual forces are released in us, when we come together in a work situation to pursue a common, functional goal. These are liberating, creative forces that are of benefit to us, simply because of our co-operative association with each other. Nevertheless, because labour is a dependent variable in the market system, most of us are dependent on others for our means of livelihood. Especially those workers who are part of large, impersonal organizations, are not in control of their own lives and tend to experience an anxious dependence, which readily breeds hostility. I am certainly aware that the work world will always be characterized by relatively impersonal, functional relationships. Most of us simply cannot expect to be known personally by those in the higher echelons of management in our firms, nor can we possibly enter into personal relationships with all those we encounter at work. Nevertheless, I am also aware that the personal and economic consequences of the insecurity and impersonality of the present work world are so unfavourable for everyone concerned (in terms of dishonesty, lying, mental and emotional strain, loss of work time and inefficiency) that the situation requires transformation.

In analyzing the work mode of presence, we have
already indicated that workers ordinarily experience
a sense of power, because they examine situations,
make decisions and appropriate materials to carry out
the projects at hand. The personal satisfaction that
results gives them a sense of their own dignity as
people and as workers. In reality, however, vast
numbers among us today experience no sense of power
and little, if any, satisfaction from what they do.
They do not have power over anything at work, nor do
they make decisions or exercise many of their higher
faculties. In taking the job, they entered into an
agreement with their employer and expected that both
the employer and themselves would receive distinct,
but just, advantages from their agreement. Thus they
feel cheated, when they see that they have been reduced to mere chattels or means of production, when
they know they will be the first factor of production
to be eliminated in time of cutback, and when they
see that they are not just being useful, but being
used. When workers see that the advantages gained by
their employers and administrators are not in proportion to what they receive, they are tempted to work
out their resentment and hostility in many ways that
are directly related to honesty and truthfulness.

Studies on work problems clearly indicate that in
order to release their hostility against "the system,"
their immediate boss and their jobs, workers steal,
lie and resort to sabotaging and disrupting the work
process in many ways. All too often, lying and theft
are employees' ways of getting back at their employers
for what they feel is being robbed from them. Theft,
in particular, is a way of gaining advantage, even
when that which is stolen is neither very valuable
nor particularly desirable. Stealing is an aggressive
way of releasing hostility and gratifying instinctual
needs without expending a great deal of effort. It
is widely practised by people on all levels of the
work force today. A recent study indicates that shoplifting alone increased by ten per cent in 1983 and
that fifty per cent of all shoplifting is done by the
employees of the establishment robbed.

Knowledge gives power. The more I know about
you, the more I am able to interact to my advantage
with you. The more I know about a thing, the more I
am able to use it effectively. Therefore, to the
extent that knowledge gives us power, lying is a way
of redistributing power. A lie increases the power

of the person who tells it over the person deceived.
Making efficient decisions can only be made on the
basis of accurate facts for which administrators ordinarily have to rely on others. By misinforming those
in authority, a worker can automatically reduce their
freedom and their capacity to choose effectively.
Objectives they want to obtain can be made to appear
unattainable, obscure or undesirable. Relevant al-
ternatives may be presented as more or less favourable
than they are in reality. In all these ways, confidence in the best choice is weakened. Estimates of
risks, costs and benefits can we varied endlessly by
deception, so that ineffective decisions are sure to
be made. Whether the means is camouflage, cover-up,
silence or deliberate deception, the effect is the
same--the loss of power and efficiency of those deceived. At worst, lies injure us in our very lives,
because they lead us astray. In fact, deception is
akin to violence; both are forms of assault that
coerce their victims unjustly. Deceit, of course,
controls more subtly than violence,because it influences both what we believe and what we do.[15]

     Whereas management regards acts of deception and
violence as attempts by workers to unjustly coerce
them, workers frequently justify their deceit and
theft as acts of self-defense and necessary means of
survival. The adversary stance between management
and labour has become so exaggerated and so widespread
that forthright, honest communication between the
various levels of management and workers is minimal.
Even in day to day communication among executives,
supervisors and foremen, many are convinced that being
truthful is not a viable option open to them. Many
people in responsible mid-management positions feel
locked into situations in which telling the truth,
either about the real control they exercise over their
workers or about numerous other facts essential for
making effective decisions, is just not a real choice
for them. They are threatened from below and above.
Laying the facts on the table might just as easily
cost them their jobs as provide them with the assistance they need to get their jobs done properly.

     If workers are going to be given any real choice
in labour disputes, they must have the same access to
all the relevant data as management, and they must
have this information simultaneously. Too frequently
people with little power in institutions are told
only what the administration wants them to know. The

facts presented may all be true and the procedure
used may be within the law, yet the scenario presented
is not the whole picture. Those with less power are
put in the position of having to make decisions
against their own best interests. If they withstand
pressure and demand more facts, a second position is
usually set forth, and so on, until agreement is
reached.

The extremes to which games, posing and one-
upmanship have gone are simply overlooked, provided
everything is within the letter of the law. What is
legal is equated unreflectively with what is moral,
and the long term consequences of what is said and
done during negotiations are too frequently disre-
garded, provided the immediate result of the action
makes those with power, in either management or
labour, look good for the moment. The moral consequences of concealing facts, especially in salary
negotiations, has got to be taken more seriously.
For instance, at the time of a cutback, an honest,
straightforward statement of a firm's financial picture, indicating the exact nature of the crisis and
showing how much personnel on all levels will be asked
to sacrifice, ought to be mandatory before people on
any level are asked to make concessions for the good
of the whole. To deliberately negotiate a very hard
contract with those with least power in an institution, on the grounds of necessity, and then, a few
months later, to negotiate a more generous contract
with those with more clout, is morally reprehensible.

Our need for certainty is one facet of our need
for security. We try to overcome uncertainty by creating new institutions that will pin things down, by
passing new laws and by adding new clauses to con-
tracts. However, to the extent that these legal realities succeed in providing security for one side of
a dispute, they are seen as ways of manipulating and
gaining the ascendancy by the other. What provides
security for one becomes a new threat to the other.
This fact alone indicates the inadequacy of a predominantly legal approach to what are predominantly personal problems. In fact, the rapidity by which we
look first to the legal consequences of alternative
responses, as soon as a new situation arises, is a
measure of how insecure and threatened we are and how
far we are from a mindset that is likely to resolve
our problems. To act legally is not necessarily to
act morally, nor is legal action a guarantee that no

one will get hurt. Thus, the capacity of legal procedures to reduce insecurity, and the hostility insecurity creates, is very limited. Honesty and truthfulness, as we have been discussing them, can be supported minimally, but not achieved, by legal means.

Even the democratization of large institutions is
no guarantee that insecurity will be reduced. In
fact, in some instances, abuse of democratization
leads to much greater insecurity, hostility and dishonesty on the part of all concerned. Too many
clever, but fundamentally deceptive executives, establish and effectively control committees that they
use to make decisions for them that directly influence
the lives of hundreds of people. Under the guise of
a democratic process of objective peer evaluation and
decision-making, these executives almost absolutize
their own power and almost eliminate their personal
accountability. This abuse of power greatly increases
the frustration and hostility of those subjected to
their authority and depersonalizes people and institutions, at the same time as personalistic concern
and values are outwardly avowed.

Too frequently, solutions to what are really personal problems are worked out in terms of technical
and economic considerations alone, with the result
that workers are disadvantaged by policies that they
are told are for their benefit. Because labour is
only one of the major factors of production, it pays
management to bring human relations techniques to
bear upon people at work. These techniques, and many
of the changes proposed by the human factors branch
of industrial engineering, are presented to workers,
as if they were for their good. Yet, at times, they
have the dual aim of enticing workers to think as
management wants them to think and of persuading them
to accept changes that, in the long run, are to their
disadvantage. This type of behaviour reflects a lack
of respect for those concerned and widens the credibility gap that already exists at most levels. Even
when nothing illegal or flagrantly dishonest is being
done, this kind of action leads workers to despair of
ever being freed from domination by "the institution."
Workers are driven toward thinking in terms of "it,"
"they," "the establishment;" and rather than moving
toward a co-operative spirit of working with management, they simply go on having to perform specified
duties. The spirit of respect, concern, honesty and
truthfulness is diminished, not fostered.

If a spirit of respect and truth is to be maintained in the work world, the fundamental otherness
of every person must be accepted and supported in
practice. No company or employer has the right to
try to change an employee by injecting its own perspective into her/him by pressure, propaganda or ma-
nipulative suggestion. The management of a company
certainly has the right to teach and try to influence
its new employees to accept and adopt, in practice,
its philosophy and company policies, provided, of
course, that it is conscientiously convinced that
these policies are just, right and truly good business. Insofar as a company's policies and philosophy
are just and good business, it has a right to influence its new employees to let them take seed and grow
in them, in the form that is suited to each of them
as people.[16] In this way, the new employees, while
retaining their own unique personalities and independence, internalize or embody the defining characteristics of the company, and so are able to propagate the
life of the company in and through their work. That
which the company stands for is made present in the
employees; but they are neither possessed nor coerced
by the company.

The confusion we experience today between rights
and obligations, and among desires, wants, needs,
aspirations and ideals, is so widespread and so destructive in both our personal and work lives that it
is hard to find a starting point to dispell it. The
use of hidden persuaders by advertizing to create
artificial needs and the deceptive innuendo that everyone has a right to almost unlimited power are but
two of the hundreds of causes of this confusion. The
subtle, but no less blatant, dishonesty and lack of
truthfulness that promote this confusion are largely
motivated by economic greed; and there is little evidence that we intend to change. Erich Fromm tells
us that sickness consists in wanting what is not
good for us. His insight is both accurate and appli-
cable. The widespread subordination of what is authentically good for us (the personal) to the promotion
of profit has gone on for so long that we don't even
recognize it, and we are not yet willing to face the
hard truths and questions that can lead to a change
in our priorities and attitudes. In the meantime,
confusion is increasing the fear, the personal and
economic insecurity and the anger and hostility of
those who see that they can't get their hands on a
very big piece of the pie. All these factors are

destroying personal presence and peace in the world
community.

Prejudice is another major personal abuse that
creates false knowledge, promotes lack of understanding and utterly destroys the possibility of mutual
presence. Prejudice creates fear and hostility, and
so inhibits people from revealing themselves openly
to each other. However, as I see it, the problem is
even more subtle than that. My prejudice toward you
is a preconceived judgment or opinion about you based
on insufficient, impersonal, inaccurate knowledge of
you. My opinion of you is subtley conveyed to you in
what I say, even when I try to conceal it and when
the content of my communication with you is primarily
functional and positive. Your response to me has got
to be based on what I have communicated to you, not
on something else, even if that something else is
more real, more true. If I am going to recognize
what you say as a response to what I have said to
you, you simply can't ignore the content of my original communication. Ordinarily, therefore, you are
not free to abstract from my prejudice and respond
independently of it, because to do so would cut off
communication with me altogether. Therefore, in a
genuine sense, in such a situation, you are forced to
respond to me from a disadvantaged position, one that
contains a real element of untruthfulness.

Even apart from your emotions toward me, my original communication to you causes your response to me
to be only partially true. It can only reveal a very
limited amount of truth about yourself and your position regarding my proposal to you. It cannot outrightly oppose the errors about yourself that I conveyed in my communication, so that what you say may
or may not confirm my original opinion of you. The
point that I wish to emphasize here is that the element of untruthfulness (the lack of reality) in both
my communication to you and your response to me tends
to take us further apart in our knowledge of each
other, rather than bringing us to a more accurate,
mutual understanding. Communication grounded on the
false foundation of prejudice tends to take us further
and further from being mutually present to each other.
Positive efforts have to be made to overcome prejudice, if ongoing communication between people is going
to reverse the tide and bring them together as people,
and not merely as functionaries.

At least on a functional level, today, people of
minority groups are allowed to interact in our whole
society in a more personal fashion than in the past.
Yet, as long as equality and respect for members of
minorities is not freely given, genuine personal presence is not achieved and personal damage is still
being done. For generations, black people and other
minorities were not permitted to express their frustration and hostility against white people and their
institutions. Thus, their hostility was turned back
on themselves and caused depression, self-hatred,
apathy and disintegration in their own communities.
The civil rights movement prevented the psychological
suicide of black Americans. Their hostility found
outlets through legal procedures, economic pressures
and other violent and nonviolent actions. Now, their
increased freedom of action and expression affords
them the opportunity to express their hostility toward white people directly. We might measure the
progress that has been made in the last decade by the
number of U.S. cities that have elected black mayors
and by the fact that a black person has found it possible to declare candidacy for the presidency. Nevertheless, as long as only a few black people have real
economic and political power, and as long as the majority do not receive respect and acceptance as
people, hostility, and undoubtedly violence against
white people, can be expected to increase.[17] This
is a regrettable fact that ought to spur white
America to face hard truths about prejudice and to
avoid the dishonesty inherent in complacency and to-
kenism. These are ways of living out a lie. Violence
needs nourishment and it obtains it from lies.

Whereas prejudice always destroys personal presence, and so ought to be eliminated, only excessive
competition is destructive of presence, honesty and
truthfulness. Thus, we need only reduce competition.
We are so used to living in what is undoubtedly the
most competitive of all civilizations that we do not
notice the excesses in work, aggressiveness, one-up
manship and all the minor acts of dishonesty that are
caused by the pressure we are under to succeed. There
was a time when business and politics were the main
arenas for competition in our society, but we have
certainly moved beyond that today. In fact, it is
difficult to find a single area of life into which
keen competition has not spread.

The grave disservice done, even to preschoolers,

by excessive competition in little league sports has been brought to our attention many times during the last ten years. Competition is used on all levels in the education process to spur students to be industrious. A child learns at a very early age that her/his advantage is the other child's disadvantage and that s/he ought to capitalize on this to get ahead. Children are taught by parents and teachers that they are expected to compete and succeed, regardless of their natural aptitude for the particular activity. Who knows how many teen-agers drop out of school because their image of themselves is threatened by excessive competition. The competition to obtain entry into university and into the program of one's choice is constantly on the increase. If grading is done on a curve, students have to compete against each other besides standing up to stiff objective standards. Where final grades are determined by the student's improvement during a course, each student finds her/himself in the unenviable position of constantly having to surpass her/his performance of the previous day or week.

Our whole education system, we are led to believe, is geared to challenge our youth and prepare them for the work world. These, of course, are necessary and noble goals; but they must be pursued in a more balanced fashion. We expend little time and energy teaching youth to complement and support each other, rather than constantly competing. Parents and educators can pressure the young into habits of relating that minimize genuine presence, because they are always looking ahead of the present moment to make the best possible move. Young people easily adopt the erroneous attitude that dishonesty and lying are a necessary part of normal living, if they are going to hold their own or get ahead. These attitudes are destructive. It is possible to demand a quality, quantity and consistency of production that is dehumanizing. Learning takes place in spurts that are separated by plateaus in which the scholar relates and assimilates what has been grasped quickly. So too, productivity in other areas is more related to the normal ebb and flow of life than to steady, mechanical output. Constant competition and emphasis on maximal productivity pressure people into dishonesty and provoke defensive lying.

The old saying that "yesterday's glories are precisely that, yesterday's" is too frequently made an

unwritten policy. When we take this approach to productivity too seriously, we devalue our past achievements and force ourselves to prove our worth anew
every day. The value of the person as such is subordinated to her/his functional worth in such a radical
way that many feel that they are left with no reasonable, honourable options. They begin to use any
strategy they can to defend themselves; their con-
sciences atrophy and they develop attitudes regarding
what constitutes truth and honesty on the basis of
their behaviour. The white lies, minor acts of deception and theft that began as defenses cannot be
contained. They perpetuate themselves and grow to
the point where, paradoxically, what originally was
justified, and provided security and a defense against
the establishment, becomes a cause of constant insecurity and fear of exposure. Similarly, although
lying may give immediate power over the person deceived, it leaves those who lied with no power at all
once their word is no longer trusted.

Monitors of ethical practices in business have
told us for years that competition is the factor with
the greatest influence on ethical behaviour in the
business world. Unethical behaviour soon arises where
there is either excessive or inadequate competition.
There is no doubt that competition is a major factor
in determining behaviour in all areas of life today.
It causes some people to become over-achievers who
get most of their personal satisfaction from success
at work-oriented activities. Thus it is easy for
them to fall into the trap of approaching most encounters from a work perspective. They run the risk of
eventually reducing most of their experience to work
experience. They put themselves on a treadmill that
deprives them of genuine, personal sharing; and so
they do not develop their potential in that area. To
the extent that their interpersonal skills remain
undeveloped, they are unconsciously motivated to work
even harder to assure at least some satisfaction in
life. Eventually, their whole life is based on a
false understanding of who they are or could become.

In a similar manner, those who are excessively
ambitious over-emphasize interactions that are dominantly competitive. In a competitive context, only
certain facets of their personalities come to the
fore and are developed. The self and competitors are
summed up from a very limited perspective and never
known in their fullness. Excessively ambitious exec-

utives and administrators easily fall prey to the
illusion that they possess extraordinary qualities of
leadership and insight, because others find it easier
to give them their way than to challenge them. If
excessive ambition is combined with a recurring need
to prove themselves, they are driven, consciously or
unconsciously, to grasp for more and more power.
When such leaders see themselves as acting in the
best interests of their institutions, they drive
excessively hard bargains and put unreasonable demands
for achievement on others. Blinded by their own ambition and their need to win and possess power to control their situation, they lose a true vision of the
goals of their institution and the personal significance of its employees. They do not give honest,
straightforward reasons for their decisions or for
policies that directly affect the lives of others.
The absence of such reasons leads employees to search
for hidden agendas and creates all the insecurity
that suspicion entails.

The experience of psychologists indicates that
when an administrator confronts an employee, in an
honest, charitable manner, with difficult truths about
her/his failure to live up to required standards, the
exchange is not taken either as a threat or as an
insult. In fact, it is likely to provide a basis for
deepened, mutual respect and friendship. Therefore,
many of the excuses given instead of real reasons,
and much of the political maneuvering thought to be
so essential to maintaining good working relations,
are counterproductive. These methods of communicating
promote the careers of ambitious executives more than
either the good of those who are supposedly being
protected or that of the institution as a whole.
Being excessively competitive or ambitious are no
more signs of strength than is a lust for power. All
three kill. They are measures of a person's weakness
and signs of a pervasive, underlying lack of honesty
at the base of her/his communication with others.
Honesty is knowing, accepting and being present to
oneself and others as one really is. These excesses
skew one's view of oneself and divert one's energies
and those of others to behaviour that detracts from
personal presence and freely chosen co-operation in
the work place.

We have put the functional before the personal on
a consistent basis. By doing so, we have backed ourselves into a corner from which we cannot even see

the possibility of reversing the tide of dishonesty,
lying and other abuses that plague our public life
and work world. We have made success and efficiency
ends in themselves; in reality, they are simply means.
Ultimately, the only adequate reason for producing
goods and providing services efficiently is to increase the quality of personal life they afford. In
order to subordinate the functional to the personal,
we must take measures to reduce the impersonality and
negative motivation in public and work life. We shall
accomplish this only if we transform our places of
work from mere associations to being as much like
communities as possible.

We form associations for specific, functional
purposes. The principle that brings the members of
an association together and maintains unity and co-
operation among them is a useful, not a personal one.
The primary purpose of the members is not to get to
know each other as people, but to co-operate with
each other as workers. That is to say, by intention,
their relation to each other is impersonal, rather
than personal; and, in many instances, their underlying motivation is likely to be negative, rather
than positive.

A community is not a unity of people as workers,
but as people. The goal of the members is sharing in
each other's lives--creating a communion or fellowship
among each other. Although functional ends, co-operation, organization and most of the other characteristics of an association are also inherent in a community, these realities neither hold a community together nor assure its viability. By intention, the
members enter into a personal relationship with each
other; and more likely than not, the underlying motivation is positive. Love, care and friendship maintain a community. Each member is respected as a
unique individual whose contribution complements that
of the other members. However, unity is not achieved
in a community by a functional union of differences.
The members develop or realize their personalities
through the functions they perform on behalf of the
group, but their primary self-realization is achieved
from their personal union with each other. In spite
of the fact that there is no equality among the members in terms of ability, skills, function and contribution, there is an intentional equality as persons.
Freedom is also a characteristic of community, because
love and friendship reduce fear and create an atmos-

phere in which the members feel free to act.[18]

We have indicated a number of times that the work world will always be characterized by some degree of impersonality. From what we have just said, it is also clear that we simply cannot transform our public institutions and places of employment from associations into communities. Nevertheless, there is no reason for us to restrict our knowledge, attitudes and relationships with each other at work to the impersonal. We can extend them to include the personal, and we can transform our places of work by having them take on many of the qualities of a community. Obviously, this has been done for years by millions of people and companies on more or less an individual basis; but, in itself, this has not proved adequate. In general, our institutions are still characterized by an impersonality that breeds fear and hostility. Labour relations operate on an adversary basis, and most people accept the negative attitudes and behaviour they encounter at work as inevitable, if not normal.

It is beyond my scope and competence to point to all the economic and managerial changes that will be required if we are to add a dimension of community to our enormous institutions. Some form of profit sharing, some degree of ownership and some means of sharing responsibility for more than a few, limited operations are already being used as a few workable means to achieve this goal. I shall suggest only a few changes in outlook and practice that will have to complement the more technical changes, if any real progress is to be achieved.

The narrow approach to education by which we train our youth to develop functional skills, in order to ensure themselves employment, has got to be expanded to include a much broader base in the humanities and in values. Education is for living more than it is for working. To say that I am a professor or a bricklayer is a much too narrow focus for anyone's vision of self today. Children have got to be educated in such a way that after years in the work world they will still be asking "what will I be when I grow up?". Life is an unending process of developing new occupational skills, becoming oneself and learning to be present to God, other people and things in deeper, more satisfying ways. The need for developing work skills and professional competence cannot be under-

estimated; but the efforts we make to help our youth
fulfill this need have to be subordinated to an extensive effort to help them achieve personal growth.
The former activity takes longer and longer, as is
evident from the number of years and degrees it takes
to prepare ourselves for suitable employment. The
latter activity takes a lifetime. Each new step toward personal growth becomes possible only when we
experience a corresponding degree of security or safety. Our present society, and particularly our work
world, are too often conterproductive in this respect.

Education in and respect for values ought to be
given top priority in all educational institutions
and in in-service programs provided for workers.
Moral education and decision-making, done in the light
of personalistic values, can effectively replace much
of our present concern for human relations education
and techniques. Today, highly trained professionals,
who have only a superficial smattering of the humanities and social sciences, are simply not capable of
providing leadership or handling managerial or per-
sonnel-related jobs effectively. The transformation
or conversion in the work world we are advocating
cannot occur if our leaders are not as equally committed to fostering humanistic values as they are to
being efficient and making a profit.

Respect for honesty and truthfulness, recognized
as goods in themselves and as necessary conditions
for the success of any collective undertaking, need
to be instilled in the work force. This process will
have to be achieved primarily by example; and it is
clear that this will only be forthcoming as the work
atmosphere changes from an impersonal milieu, in which
defensive lying and theft are justified, to one in
which mutual love and respect are genuine. In setting
forth the biblical concept of truth, we saw the inherent connection between love and truth. Love is
truthful, and one cannot cling to and continually try
to express truth without love. To love is to will
the good of the other. This does not require a great
deal of personal knowledge of those involved; there
is no possibility for that. However, it does require
a willingness to listen to the real needs of others,
an honest acknowledgement of their best interests,
and a sincere effort to see that these are effectively
promoted to the extent that this is possible. Impersonality, power, fear and hostility kill. Genuine
concern, and the honest communication it fosters, can

become the ground on which we can create new life in the work place.

It is not unrealitic to say that charity can become both the motor and brakes of our economic decision-making. Without doubt, charity includes love of the profit and success that keep our enterprises economically viable; but it also includes love of employees and customers. The will to promote their good and satisfy their needs should fuel our economic enterprises as much as our desire for profit. On the other hand, when pressures on employees become too great, when the alternative is either laying off workers or accepting an economically feasible (but not appealing) loss of profit, or when a thousand other variables occur that are really not for the good of workers or those serviced by our enterprises, it is charity that ought to move us to apply the brakes and make decisions with everyone's interests in mind.

The verb "to respect" is derived from the Latin *respicere* which means to look at or to notice. The respect that workers on all levels demand today is to be seen or looked at as people, not as mere objects or instruments of production. Once again, this does not require that those in management know their employees individually. That is impossible. However, it does require that all of us make a sincere effort to curb the impersonality that pervades our places of work and that we treat each other with the consideration due to personal subjects.

First, management and labour will have to co-operate with each other to create an atmosphere in which they can meet, not as adversaries, but as people trying to be open and receptive to each other's perspectives, needs and best interests. Only in such an atmosphere of respect and co-operation will both sides be able to acknowledge their mutual interdependence without fear of one taking undue advantage of the other. The false air of independence exhibited so often by both sides in labour disputes is more indicative of immaturity and insecurity than manliness. After that fleeting moment during which teen-agers experience total independence from their parents, if their growth is to continue, they go on to develop a relationship with them that involves healthy, mutual interdependence. The facade of independence put up by negotiators in work disputes injures everyone concerned, in the same way as lying and theft injure

those who perform such acts and those who are victim-
ized. The effects of continued deception are cumula-
tive and hard to reverse, because lack of trust becomes more and more ingrained.

When people on all echelons in the work world
acknowledge by their actions that they respect each
other's dignity and equality as people, positive motives will have a better chance to replace the negative motives that predominate at present. Since
negative motivation promotes self-interest and individualism, for defensive reasons, its replacement by
more co-operative motives will not only bring about a
transformation in the way those concerned are present
to each other, it may even have beneficial consequences on their productivity.

To be genuinely personal, relationships must be
positive and inclusive. Yet, we have seen that, by
intention, impersonality, which is negative and exclusive, dominates our places of employment. The
satisfaction and self-realization of workers, on the
one hand, and their efficiency and productivity, on
the other, are both being impeded in the present situation. Surely, then, the modifications I am advocating cannot be set aside as either unnecessary or
unrealistic.

Notes

1. Macmurray, pp. 65-67.
2. Ibid., p. 64.
3. Ibid., p. 68.
4. Ibid., p. 69.
5. Ibid., pp. 69-70.
6. Ibid., pp. 70-71.
7. Ibid., p. 71.
8. Ibid., pp. 71-72.
9. Ibid., pp. 73-74.
10. Ibid., pp. 74-75.
11. Ibid., P. 149.
12. Ibid., p. 150.
13. Ibid., p. 102.
14. Ibid., pp. 103-05.
15. Sissela Bok, *Lying: Moral Choice in Public and
Private Life*, (New York: Random House, Vintage Books,
1978), pp. 19-21.
16. Martin Buber, "Distance and Relation," *The*

Knowledge of Man, p. 69.

17. Frederick Herzberg, *The Managerial Choice: To Be Efficient and To Be Human*, (Homewood, Ill.: Dow Jones-Irwin, 1976), pp. 19-21.

18. Macmurray, pp. 157-58.

PART FOUR

CREATING A FUTURE IN THE PRESENCE OF GOD

Chapter 6

TOWARD A MORE PERSONALISTIC FUTURE

From Short to Long Term Pragmatism

A large percentage of North Americans would certainly disavow pragmatism as their philosophy of life.
Yet, a serious look at the way most of us make decisions in virtually all facets of our lives reveals
that we are a pragmatic people. We think pragmati-
cally and act on the basis of decisions that have
been made on pragmatic considerations, whether we are
aware of it or not. We are also influenced, to a great
extent, by pragmatic criteria for attaining truth. It
is reasonable, therefore, that if we are going to
transform our society into a more personalistic one,
we must start by attempting to understand our present.
pragmatic approach to reality. After all, any future
we try to create will have to be built out of the
present. Thus, it seems to me, that we must attain a
clearer understanding of those aspects of pragmatic
theory that concern its criteria for truth and the
distinction between pragmatic and utilitarian thought
and practice. At present, we approach reality and,
too frequently, attempt to solve our problems from
the perspective of a short term pragmatism that is
akin to utilitarianism.

John Dewey is the American philosopher who developed to its fullest expression the pragmatic understanding of inquiry, meaning and truth.1 For Dewey,
the pragmatic approach highlights practicality, but
does not equate what is practical with what is simply
useful or utilitarian. Pragmatism is not utilitarianism. Both the pragmatic approach to inquiry and
its criteria for truth emphasize the need to refer to
consequences as the meaning and test of all thinking.
Since the consequences of an action extend to the

moral, esthetic, religious and political dimensions of our lives, as well as to what is useful, we can never restrict pragmatic consideration of consequences to what is useful or to what promotes material well-being alone. In determining the validity of a goal, event or action in terms of its consequences, we are never justified in reducing our considerations to either immediate or even long term usefulness. The most significant consequences of our goals and actions are those that affect us specifically as persons, that is to say, consequences that develop character and personality or those that fragment us. Thus, genuine pragmatic considerations must extend beyond consequences that can be measured in terms of utility.

For instance, the difference between the utilitarian and pragmatic approaches to meaning and value comes into sharp focus when they are applied to the act of martyrdom, an action that has been held in esteem throughout the Hebrew and Christian traditions. Martyrdom is the act of giving up one's life to maintain one's integrity by bearing witness to the validity of a principle or truth. If the only criterion by which we judge this act is utility, it is hardly possible to justify it at all, let alone perceive it as the only moral alternative in some circumstances. Nevertheless, according to the pragmatic criterion of examining all the forseeable consequences of the alternative choices available, some people may well regard accepting martyrdom as the only moral choice available to them in a particular situation.

Throughout history, many people have been forced into either facing execution or performing an act which, in their conscientious judgment, would fragment them and destroy their personal integrity. According to pragmatic criteria, a person in such a situation may conscientiously decide that to perform the action demanded of her/him would be equivalent to destroying her/himself. In other words, the consequences of carrying out the act would be tantamount to death. Thus, accepting death at the hands of another could be seen as the only meaningful and moral alternative available. In this situation, where destruction is inevitable, a person may very reasonably decide, on the basis of good, clear pragmatic reasoning, that it is better to maintain her/his personal integrity and exercise her/his freedom by choosing to be destroyed by another, than to perform an act that would destroy her/himself.

This illustration demonstrates that what we ordinarily regard to be genuine, pragmatic thinking is
much more restricted and restrictive than what is
proposed to us by Dewey's theory. We have already
discussed the biblical understanding of truth at
length. Now we shall complement that approach by a
discussion of the pragmatic criteria of truth. This
discussion will enable us to see how much our daily
practice falls short of living up to pragmatic
criteria. It will also reveal why a move away from a
short, toward a long term pragmatism, is important,
if we are to develop a more personalistic future.
Historically, three basic theories of truth have been
developed: the coherence theory, the correspondence
theory and the pragmatic theory. These theories have
distinct, yet also overlapping criteria for truth;
and are often combined, so that criteria from all
three theories are used together.2 In my estimation,
it is in this combined context that the pragmatic
criteria are most frequently used and most helpful.

For the pragmatist, ideas, meanings and theories
are instruments people use in actively understanding
and reorganizing problematic situations. The test of
their validity lies in their ability to resolve the
particular situation at hand. If they succeed, they
are reliable or true; if not, they are false. The
verification of an idea or a theory lies in the consequences it brings about; that which guides a process
of interaction in such a way as to bring about the
best possible set of consequences is the true solution
for that situation. We see, therefore, that truth,
in the pragmatic context, is often discussed in terms
of satisfaction. The satisfaction at stake concerns
the needs and conditions of the specific problem out
of which the idea or plan of action we decide is the
true one arose. It involves objective conditions,
and can never be reduced to either a personal, emotional satisfaction or comfort or to the gratification
of a strictly personal need or profit. The element
of correspondence inherent in the pragmatic theory is
a dynamic adjustment between the consequences foreseen
as the result of the plan of action projected to rec-
tify the situation and the actual consequences or
conditions brought forth by the application of this
plan in the concrete situation.

Pragmatic theory maintains that truths arrived at
in solving one problem are effective in similar situations, so that they become permanent resources that

are relatively unchanging. Thus, this approach acknowledges a certain permanent status to truth, while
at the same time maintaining that truth is incomplete,
always inherently limited and in process of development. This ongoing quality of truth, as expressed in
pragmatic theory, is compatible with the primary criterion of the coherence theory. The truth of an idea
or theory lies in its power to develop itself indefinitely without internal contradictions. A true theory
forms a positive whole in which the parts complement
and support each other. Thus, the more true one's
vision of reality, the more its various elements continue to illuminate each other indefinitely, so that
wider, formerly unseen horizons present themselves
for future inquiry. True scientific discovery consists in finding hidden connections between areas and
orders that previously appeared to be unrelated.

North Americans frequently misunderstand and
rather consistently misapply the pragmatic approach
to determining the value and truth of concepts, ideas
and methods of inquiry. As a result, we have created
an environment in which genuine personal presence,
honesty and truthfulness have been hindered, rather
than fostered. Our tendency to equate pragmatic with
utilitarian criteria has drastically narrowed the
range of consequences that we ordinarily consider in
our decision-making and in determining the value and
truth of our actions and ideas. The value of a thing
cannot be determined in terms of its utility alone.
There is a vast range of activities and things that
give meaning and purpose to our lives that are not
useful. Their value extends beyond the realm of utility and the common need, yet they are so essential to
the common good that civilized society cannot exist
without them. Art, music, beauty, religion, philosophy and the whole tradition of the liberal arts fall
within this category.

Our pragmatic deliberations also fail to foster
presence, honesty and truthfulness in our society as
a whole. As individuals and groups, we make our deliberations without adequate consideration of the
whole range of personal consequences that result from
our actions and with little consideration of the consequences for those beyond our own particular interest
group. Pragmatism is thought to justify the narrow
calculation that centers on our own self-interest and
profit. In reality, it condemns such behaviour.

In a similar vein, we usually think that the truth of an hypothesis or theory is validated if a successful technological invention can be developed from it. In fact, inadequately developed theories, with numerous flaws, often have beneficial spinoff effects. Their usefulness in this regard is no guarantee of their truth. The truth of a theory, as we have already seen, is determined in terms of its ability to extend itself indefinitely without developing inherent contradictions. This standard extends beyond utility. Thus, we see that the pragmatic quality of truth is more accurately conceived in terms of a much broader productiveness (including the specifically human) than in terms of either useful or predominantly material criteria.

An equally serious limitation, prevalent in our practice of pragmatic decision-making, is our tendency to examine things in terms of their short, rather than their long term consequences. Any pragmatic practice that is going to be successful on an ongoing basis must include its own process of examining the present and projecting more pervasive, far-reaching (but concrete) objectives and goals for action. Our weakness in this regard is making decisions in the light of short term objectives and immediate consequences for ourselves alone, rather than in terms of more far-reaching consequences for all the people and/or nations that will benefit or suffer from our actions.

Modern electronic technology provides us with new tools or instruments never before available to mankind. However, tools do not decide the purposes for which they will be used. We determine the ideals or ends to which to direct technological advances. Technology has ideal value only insofar as we use it to enable us to gain control of and direct the processes that help us achieve the values that give meaning to our lives. The mass communication networks formed through television and telstar have created one, massive nervous system and common consciousness for the whole of humanity. These can be used to enable people of entirely different backgrounds to share each other's culture and to be personally present to each other in ways never before possible. We have much of the technology now that is required to provide the material base for a world community. High tech, in fact, enables us to project previously unimagined ideals and goals that can help to solve pressing

human, social problems all over the world. Yet, we
continue to subject instruments that could liberate
us to our old, narrow, individualistic, nationalistic
and profit motives with insufficient regard for the
genuine personal and social benefits that could be
achieved by them. The consequences of many of our
short term policies interfere with each other, the
disadvantages of one erasing the benefits of another.
The result is conflict, divisiveness and the destruction of personal presence.

We commit ourselves to political, economic, social
and even marital relationships only to the extent
that the consequences for us correspond with precisely
what we want. The moment we realize that we shall
have to put more and more of our personal resources,
time and energy into these relationships if we are to
reap the rewards we want, we feel perfectly justified
in withdrawing from them, regardless of the consequences for others. Freedom is frequently the only
moral value we are willing to recognize as relevant
to these situations, and sometimes we deny that whole
areas of life have anything to do with morality at
all. In contrast to this, pragmatic theory emphasizes
that there are no areas of life outside the realm of
morality. A clear-cut distinction between a set of
moral goods or virtues and a separate set of natural
goods (health, art and science), which we are free to
pursue without moral constraint, is invalid. Every
facet of our lives is open to moral scrutiny. In the
light of pragmatic standards, therefore, we can no
longer feel morally free to enter and withdraw from
relationships without serious consideration of the
long term consequences for all those concerned.

Surely, over the past twenty years, our painful
experiences in the areas of ecology, urban renewal
and the distribution of limited resources have taught
us that our moral deliberations must be more comprehensive, more interrelated and unified and directed
toward more and more inclusive aims. Experience is
teaching us to seek our satisfactions and our self-
realization in goals that bring satisfaction and self-
realization to others. What we have overlooked in
pragmatic theory, namely, that general or universal
thought is at the same time generous thought, must be
given its rightful place in our consciousness and
practice. The tremendous complexity of our social,
political and economic interactions today has greatly
increased both the radius of action of most members

of our society and the power of mutual penetration of
all its members. We influence each other in ways
people never dreamed of in the past. Our interaction
is so complex that we can no longer pursue our own
interests without regard for the consequences to
others and hope that somehow a spirit of community
and the good of our whole society will be fostered.

I propose that we must shift from short to long
term pragmatic considerations and policies, if we are
going to create an atmosphere in which we can effectively foster genuine, personal presence and community. However, before I make specific recommendations
for change to a long term perspective, I shall say
something about ideals.3 This is essential, because
what we mean by ideals, and how we set about to establish and live by them, are intimately connected with
this change to a long term perspective and with promoting presence and community.

First, it is essential to acknowledge that our
ideals are ongoing and in need of constant reevalu-
ation. Technological and social advances force us to
reexamine the meaning, application and consequences
of even our most constant, comprehensive long term
ideals as well as our immediate, specific ones. Let
me give an example. Peace, which is closely connected
with personal presence, is a constant ideal cherished
by the vast majority of people on this continent.
Yet, if I am not mistaken, a rather radical change in
our understanding of peace and the way it is attained
has taken place since the fifties. At that time we
tended to understand peace as flowing from the inherent structures of things and institutions in society.
We placed a great deal of emphasis on relatively permanent structures that had a given place in society.
Their functioning was seen to create peace. We recognized a certain calm and stability to peace; it was
somewhat static, something created and enforced by
structures, law and order. Although somewhat of an
overstatement, peace, as we understood it then, could
be achieved when the institutions of society performed
their proper functions and when people adhered to the
old saying "a place for everything [and everybody],
and everything [and everybody] in its place."

Hiroshima and Nagasaki caused the beginnings of
serious rumblings that the means of war had changed
qualitatively and that war and the just war theory
were open to serious questions. The Vietnam war cre-

ated innumerable questions and problems, until it was finally acknowledged to be unworkable. Vatican II stirred up the waters and changed the meaning and place of religious liberty, the laity and the Church itself. The civil rights movement, the women's and gay liberation movements, among others, demanded that society adapt almost immediately to give new places to people and their rights. A major consequence of living through all the tensions created by these changes has been the slow emergence of a richer understanding of peace itself and the way to go about achieving it.

Today, we understand peace as the result of fidelity to ongoing, harmonious relations among people, fidelity to interactions that are established and maintained primarily by justice. This new understanding still acknowledges that peace is the fruit of order, but the order that creates peace is not a static order imposed by those in authority or by the military or by law. The order that promotes peace is an ongoing harmony based upon respect for people expressed concretely in terms of freedom, justice, truth and love.[4] This is a much more dynamic concept than the one we accepted a few years ago. It places more emphasis on change, personal presence and sharing of life as the sources and foundation of peace than it does on structures or law and order.

This illustration demonstrates many things. What concerns us here is the fact that our ideals are ongoing and that their meaning and application are in need of regular evaluation. To understand how developing and evaluating ideals takes place, let us focus on the connection between the actual or present and the ideal. The objects and interactions that constitute our present situation are to some extent problematic, yet they have value as they are. At the same time, however, they are open to further development and so to the possibility of increasing their value. Our actual situation, therefore, is really a set of conditions with which we can interact so as to create or build the most favourable future possible. When we think out the real possibilities that can be developed out of or used as methods to improve our present situation, we are developing and applying ideals. The ideal, therefore, is the possible. It is the best possible outcome or set of conditions that we can develop out of the actual or the present. The ideal can also be conceived as the idea or the true plan of

action we can use to create the future set of conditions we value most highly. The ideal is like the
right road in the biblical sense, that road that will
lead us to our goal.

We have no reason to establish opposition between
idealism and realism or between the material and the
ideal. Ideals are born out of present reality. It is
the possibility we have to interact with and in our
present material conditions that makes ideals possible. Too frequently, we regard ideals as if they
exist a step beyond the possible, as if they are somehow imposed on us from some superior realm beyond our
own. All too often we are asked to strive after
ideals that are beyond our real possibilities. Every
child is encouraged to attend university and all those
graduating are told that they can become president.
This false approach to ideals creates an atmosphere
of dishonesty.

It is not possible for any of us, and especially
youth, to be genuinely present to and accepting of
ourselves as we are (to be honest with ourselves) and
at the same time strive for unreal ideals that are
beyond our capacity. Rather than being genuinely present to ourselves, we become alienated both from ourselves and from those who propose such ideals. As a
result of our failure to achieve unattainable ideals,
we give up on ideals altogether and frequently revert
to a gross materialism. Truth, honesty and genuine
mutual presence can only be fostered in a milieu in
which we realistically assess our possibilities, select as our ideal the alternative with the most favourable long term consequences for everyone concerned, and then strive to achieve it. Taking into
consideration the reality of grace, as part of the
potential available to all those open to God's assistance, makes this approach to ideals extremely
open-ended. It assures more success than the false
approach mentioned above, and is a much more honest
way of establishing realistic aspirations and ideals.

Now that we have gained some insight into the
meaning of realistic ideals and how we can establish
them, we can recommend a few long term ideals that
will do a great deal to promote personal presence and
develop community in our society. The first is to
create a community in which people tell the truth in
their daily affairs. We deceive ourselves about the
seriousness of the consequences of the lying we en-

counter every day. We pay little attention to the massive brainwashing and deceptiveness that are part and parcel of advertizing. We pretend to be offended when accusations of deliberate lying are levelled against our political and military leaders. A Manhattan court official said to me once, "One or other of the parties in every case that comes before this court is lying." Given the fact that people perceive and interpret reality differently, surely that is an exaggeration. Nevertheless, it gives an indication of the disregard for even perjury in our society.

Many people are willing to take the risks involved in lying with the hope of short term gain and all of us go on bearing the unfavourable consequences of their behaviour. Yet we are unwilling to make the consequences for offenders sufficiently serious that lying will no longer pay. Sisela Bok has indicated very clearly that cynicism and the inability to believe in truth are ultimately the effects of constantly being subjected to lies and deception. As we destroy respect for and the experience of truth, we destroy the sense by which we establish our bearings in the real world. Trust is a social good that must be protected just as much as the air we breathe and the water we drink. When we injure trust, the community as a whole suffers, and when community is destroyed, society collapses.5 Creating a society in which lying bears serious penalties and telling the truth is expected is not an unrealistic ideal. It is that without which personal presence is impossible.

Full employment is a second, exceedingly difficult and very controversial ideal that must be taken much more seriously than at present. Full employment is intimately associated with the understanding of person as a relational being and with personal dignity. For these reasons it is essential. Let me explain more fully. We established at the outset that the basic unit in society is not a person in isolation, but a person in relation to other people. One can neither become nor know oneself apart from interactions with others. In other words, communication and participation are that without which there can be no human life. The right to be able to work, to participate in some form of interaction that will enable us to earn our means of livelihood, is as fundamental a right as the right to free speech and free association. Human dignity is the dignity of a social being who communicates and participates in the ongoing interactions of the community to the extent of her/his ability. If a person is not given the opportunity to participate in the life of the community by working, s/he is set aside and denied human dignity. We can no longer circumvent the truth that, for people capable of working, having a job is absolutely a requirement for the exercise of their freedom and for justice. Few things are more destructive and have more pervasive, negative consequences for a person than an extended period of unemployment.

It may appear totally unrealistic to even propose full employment as a possible ideal in the light of automation and an economy in which labour is one of the only factors of production to be had in abundance. Economic conditions will undoubtedly remain such that it is impossible to provide everything that is beneficial for everyone, and trade offs will continue to be necessary. Nevertheless, if personal freedom, dignity and justice are to operate at all in our society, we have to make the radical changes demanded of us by the undeniable truth that people have a right to work. Whatever we have to do to produce an economic system that delivers the right to work has to be done. The moral and social consequences of present policies that leave high unemployment rates in all sectors of the population, and up to nearly fifty percent among youth in some minorities, are so disastrous that they can no longer be tolerated.

In close connection with the right to work is the fundamental right of workers to organize. Anyone with a minimal knowledge of the labour movement on this continent knows the painful struggle that workers have had to establish this right in practice. It comes as a tremendous shock to hear that an estimated five hundred million dollars was spent on "union busting" in North America in 1983. This behaviour is morally unacceptable and a tremendous setback in terms of establishing genuine co-operation among employers and employees and creating a semblance of community in the work place. It is impossible to see how it can serve any segment of society in the long run, because it is so destructive of mutual respect and personal presence between management and labour.

The last suggestions I shall make deal with a movement toward long term policies in capital investment, production and industrial planning in general. It was interesting to note that at a recent convention on ethics in business a number of top executives from major industries mentioned that there is an awareness in the business world of the serious disadvantages of the short term policies that are so common today. They also maintained that steps are being taken to impel executives to take a longer view in their planning. Efforts are being made to alter capital raising policies, so as to enhance a shift in this direction, and management itself is being given economic remuneration for longer term productive policies, rather than for policies oriented toward immediate gain.

Other industrial leaders agreed that we live increasingly in a world economic community, so that setting business policies in terms of one's own national economy alone is becoming more and more shortsighted. They acknowledged the need for long term vision and an international perspective, regardless of the almost insurmountable obstacles in putting these into practice. A few of the hurdles that have to be overcome before long term planning can become a reality are (a) a strong reluctance to share information, (b) an emphasis on competition to the detriment of concensus building, and (c) a tendency to allow those involved in decision-making to set forth recommendations before all the parties involved agree on the facts. When this is done, people on different sides of the issue tailor the facts to fit their own recommendations. Real communication is cut short and the compromise reached is less satisfying than it could be.

We have acknowledged the pragmatic tendencies that are part of North Americans; and, by explaining pragmatic theory concerning consequences, truth and ideals, shown where some of the obstacles to personal presence and community can be overcome, as we strive toward a more personalistic future. As we spend less and less time producing the necessities of life, the unforeseen and the ideal occupy our minds and hearts more and more. The concentration that had to be focused on well-being in the past is being shifted to more-being, to being better and being more conscious. These ideals encompass all that promotes personal presence in the fullest sense. We can pursue these goals successfully only if we balance our appreciation of and need to cling to the goods we possess at the moment with a willingness to let go of them to pursue greater personal goods, not yet clearly foreseen. We have indicated that this is done each day by creating

the best possible tomorrow out of today. Now let us
look at this same process from a different perspective, the personalization of time, and in so doing,
further develop and tie together many of the themes
we have been discussing.

The Personalization of Time

There is a much more fruitful way of looking at
the present moment than thinking of it simply in terms
of fleeting minutes. The present takes on real meaning
when we understand it as presence, the personal presence of God to people and of people to each other. As
indicated earlier, personal presence is a matter of
choice or freedom. We choose the way and the degree
to which we communicate with each other. Even in the
most superficial encounters, where we freely interact
to further a goal that is of mutual interest to us,
there can be a degree of mutual presence and communication between us. An initial word of welcome by one
person is an invitation to another to respond in a
way that leaves the door open for a further reply,
one which can be genuinely personal at the same time
as it furthers the functional transaction at hand.
Where there is at least a minimum of openness, sincerity and receptivity, there is also some degree of
concern and respect. These qualities are basic requirements for personal presence and for keeping interpersonal interactions ongoing. Therefore, when we
try to live the present moment in the presence of
each other, it becomes a dialogue out of which we can
build a future in which we can continue to relate
with mutual benefit and to which we can commit ourselves.

It is rewarding personally to conceive of each
moment of our work day as an opportunity to be personally present either to those we meet directly or
to those we serve by processing some form of paper
work or providing a thousand other kinds of service.
Even when there is no direct personal encounter, it
is possible, with a bit of effort, to remind ourselves
that those we serve are real people. When we think of
what we do as part of an ongoing dialogue with those
we serve, our activities become much more personal
and rewarding. In this context, everyone shares a
mutual responsibility to keep the dialogue going and
to understand and promote, at least to the extent

that justice requires, the needs of all the other
parties. This approach fosters empathy and mutual
understanding, which in turn promote commitment, fidelity and a spirit of community. Conceiving our present activities in this way will help to create an
atmosphere in which we shall want to continue to interact with each other willingly, not simply out of
necessity.

In this context, every moment in our lives will
take on a richer meaning, since it will be understood
as an opportunity to be personally present to other
people. Our places of work will take on a new atmosphere and our jobs themselves will be transformed.
The products manufactured and/or services rendered
will become the foundation for an exchange between
us. Serving others in this situation will become an
experience of brotherhood, and the hardships involved
in interacting with our fellow workers and getting
our products or services to our clients will give
reality to friendship. In this personal context, work
will give friendship a reality and friendship will
give work an added meaning and, therefore, a real
interest. Hardships will take on meaning as an inevitable part of providing the services we provide.
They need not be experienced as simply meaningless
hassle. Technical problems, and even most of our personal ones, will remain; but they will lose many of
their burdensome, debilitating effects, because in
what we shall be doing (in the work itself) we shall
be encountering and experiencing each other as people,
not as mere functionaries. In the sharing of life we
shall experience, the personal quality of our lives
will be enhanced.

It is in efforts to bring about a real transformation in the work world that we do or live the biblical truth that people are sisters and brothers called
to use their talents to build a community of friendship and peace on earth. Truth and personal presence
become real in our lives only when we throw ourselves
into the process of incarnating them in what we are
and do. We do not simply speak the truth; we live it
and receive it in our relationships with others as
life.

Once we develop the mindset of looking at time in
terms of opportunities to be present to each other,
the present moment (time and life) become extremely
personal, and therefore something to which we can

commit ourselves wholeheartedly. It is much easier to commit ourselves to people and their service than to abstract ideas, systems, institutions or even our jobs conceived abstractly as responsibilities for which we are remunerated. Time and situations will continue to change at a tremendous rate and people will enter and leave our lives as usual. Nor will we be able to cling to the present for either meaning or security, because our way of being present now will give way to successive moments in which we shall be present to other people in different ways and degrees. Nevertheless, the present, and our personal experience of it, will never be really lost; because, as we have seen, personal presence creates an ongoing dialogue through which we build our future.

When time is conceived in terms of personal presence, many problems are seen in a new light and people's responsibilities can be more easily defined. For instance, the perennial problem as to whether our responsibility is to concentrate attention on the present or on the future can be resolved. For centuries, some have emphasized commitment to the present moment at the expense of the future, and others have sacrificed the present in order to commit themselves to the future. In the context we are proposing, responsibility is using one's ability to freely respond, and one responds to the presence of people here and now in situations that need alteration or improvement. Thus, our responsibility is to commit ourselves completely to the present moment, rather than to the future. That is to say, we commit ourselves to being present to ourselves and to our neighbours--to their aspirations and needs and to God's presence in them --in such a way that we share, work and live with them. Out of this working together and sharing, we shall build a future in which we can continue to develop ourselves and live in peace.

By following this approach we commit ourselves to neither the present nor the future exclusively, nor to one at the expense of the other. We take responsibility for the future at the same time as we act responsibly in the present. If we commit ourselves to the satisfactions of the present in a way that disregards the future consequences of our actions, we act irresponsibly. Yet, on the other extreme, disregarding the needs and satisfactions of the present, in an excessive manner, in order to assure a particular desired future, is also destructive. We cannot continually deny ourselves reasonable satisfactions in the present to assure success in the future. If we do, we end off never really living and enjoying the present moment in order to assure a more satisfying life in a future we never really allow to come into existence. Our whole lives become unsatisfying. Thus, the only responsible approach is to live the present moment with others as fully as possible, so as to build the best possible future that can be created out of it.

Irresponsibility is not merely wasting the present moment. It is not making ourselves present to others in what we say and do in such a way as to invite communication from them and receive their personal contributions. Irresponsibility is not co-operating with others in mutual endeavours to foster human life and community. We began this book by asserting that no person is an island. Our lives are not so private that we can do with our abilities whatever we choose. Nor can we arbitrarily choose to respond to or ignore chances to share our time, talents and possessions with others. All of us are responsible to open ourselves and, when the occasion arises, be willing to make sacrifices on behalf of people and developments that are far beyond the radius of our ordinary activities and interests. We simply have to keep expanding our horizons, so as to make ourselves more present to the whole. Isolationism and/or tunnel vision become increasingly irresponsible as the destiny of individuals and nations becomes more inextricably dependent on the destiny of the whole.

In this context, our responsibilities increase as our technological, social, psychological and spiritual resources increase. We are capable of being and doing that which was beyond the capabilities of our forefathers. Thus, we are responsible to use our new abilities to respond to the needs of the whole world community that we are creating by our advanced technologies. Talk of transforming the work world from a place of excessive competition, unnecessary aggressiveness and the abuse of power to a milieu in which co-operation and service rank top priority is not pious exhortation. Nor is the effort to expand the consciousness of ordinary people to include awareness of the concerns of those of other cultures and continents a utopian dream. Without moral growth in these areas now, we shall be unprepared to cope with the realities of the future world community we are creating at a very rapid pace.

Before either the reasonableness or urgency of
what I am saying about our continuously expanding
responsibilities will be acceptable to many, there
will have to be a rather radical change in attitude
and understanding of a few very fundamental realities.
The first of these is freedom. Freedom is not the
right to do whatever we feel like doing. It is one of
our highest possessions and values, because it liberates us from that which coerces and limits us, so
that we can become our true selves. In the final chapter of this book I shall discuss the fullest Christian
significance of freedom. At present, I shall simply
repeat that it is liberation from what coerces and
fragments us, from what isolates us and prevents us
from interacting successfully with others. We are
free when we do not experience obstacles, whether
interior or exterior, that prevent us from carrying
out those activities that enable us to achieve our
self-realization in communion with others. We forget
that doing what we want, when it obstructs our self-
realization, or that of others, and when it divides
rather than unites, is an abuse rather than an exercise of freedom.

We misunderstand freedom when we equate or relate
it too closely with individualism. This erroneous
approach to freedom overlooks the relational, communal
aspect of the human person that makes the basic unit
of society an individual-in-relation to others, rather
than an individual-in-isolation. As individuals, we
are thoroughly emergent from the community in which
we develop. We are free when we willingly see and
grasp those opportunities that foster our authentic
self-realization. Fulfillment that is authentic always
has a communal dimension, because the self-actualizing
person is one who contributes of her/his abundance to
the community.

A second facet of life that needs to be understood
in a different light is the role of suffering and
hardship. The shallow philosophy that advocates
avoiding suffering and hardship at all cost and promotes comfort as one of our greatest goods is simply
false. Suffering and hardship are certainly not to be
thought of as goods in themselves. Where possible, it
is our responsibility to alleviate them. Nevertheless, there is a great deal of suffering in life that
can neither be overcome nor avoided.

In analyzing the dynamic involved in human experience, John Dewey sets forth three stages: an initial encounter, a process of interaction with that which has been encountered, and thirdly, (if the second phase has been carried to its completion), a consummation that enriches the subject. The interaction between the person and that which is experienced comes to a consummation only if there is a balance achieved between acting and being acted upon. That is to say, in any experience, we perform some specific motion by which we act on or with the reality we are experiencing, and at the same time, listen, open ourselves to and allow the reality being experienced to act upon us. This element of passivity or being acted upon is a form of suffering. We suffer ourselves to be acted upon by other things and people in order to achieve a richer interaction and integration with them. Suffering is not alien, but integral, to our experience in such a way that we cannot bring our experience to a consummation or fulfillment without it. Therefore, without suffering there is no personal growth. We can neither be present to others without inconvenience, sacrifice and suffering, nor can we grasp the truth of the realities we experience without suffering.

In accord with this understanding of experience, we can readily see that the process by which we maintain an ongoing presence with our authentic selves is also a struggle involving hardship and suffering. At any stage of development, every person is a relatively unified center incorporating within her/himself meanings and values that form a view of reality that has its own unity. Everyone strives to maintain inner harmony and a balanced view of reality, but harmony and vision are not static realities. They cannot be achieved once and for all. We are constantly confronted with new ideas and different values, some of which are so opposed to our own self-image and values that they cannot be accepted. As we try to maintain an ongoing balance between our own, inner harmony and harmony with our personal, social and work environments, we find we must resist certain ideas and values, assimilate others and expand and even reorganize our view of reality. This process is painful, but there is neither honesty, truthfulness nor presence to either ourselves or others without it. Any attempt to shy away from the hardships involved in this process is serious irresponsibility, because it results in the collapse of our true selves as personal centers.

Flight from responsible personal existence is a more common cause of a pervasive dishonesty and lack of truthfulness at the core of our personalities than we ordinarily wish to acknowledge. Buber indicates that because we are unwilling to answer for the genuineness of our existence, we flee into either the general collective, which dissolves our responsibility (everybody is doing it), or a god-like position, which puts us beyond accountability (I don't have to answer to anyone but myself). These stances are extremely irresponsible. Eventually they render us incapable of listening to and acknowledging the claims of others on an equal basis. We reduce others to objects, and personal presence in any adequate sense becomes impossible.[6]

To the extent that we have forfeited our authentic selves to avoid responsibility and the hardships that are an inherent part of personal growth, conceiving of the present in terms of genuine presence to others is alien to us. Making sacrifices today on behalf of a distant future, that cannot be clearly defined and guaranteed, is even further from our horizon. To some extent at least, there is a very pervasive dishonesty in us that we mask by game playing and posing in positions that are more convenient than authentic. To look within ourselves for answers is painful and implies becoming concerned, making commitments and taking responsibility for our actions. To bring about a transformation of this magnitude in our society will require at least a very dynamic image of what it is to be human in our ongoing world. We shall only learn to enjoy responsibility (a) after we have learned to see ourselves differently, and (b) when we experience responsibility as a challenge coming from within ourselves, one from which we can obtain greater satisfaction than we are experiencing at present.

A short time ago we indicated that it is impossible to cling to the present moment. We also pointed out that no moment in life is ever really lost, because it becomes part of an ongoing dialogue out of which we build our future. In this context, where time is regarded in terms of personal presence, our past assumes its full importance in the present. My past interactions with God and with my parents, my family, my friends and even my environment become a part of me. I am my history. My personal interactions with God and other people not only constitute my past, they constitute me. That is to say, their influence on me has been internalized in the manner in which we defined personal presence at the beginning of this work. My past relationships are so much a part of me that they make me precisely who I am today. I cannot help but bring my past to my present in a very real, dynamic way.

It is foolish to try to ignore or deny our past; we can only acknowledge it and build on its foundations. Attempting to cut ourselves off from our past will guarantee that we make the same mistakes over again. It is also impossible to return to the past, because our intervening experiences have changed us and our situation. However, we can re-incorporate earlier values we have been temporarily overlooking into the present in a new way.

In the light of what has been said, we can gain further insight into the density and importance of the present moment. It sums up our past, and it is that out of which we have to call forth our future. As is indicated in the scripture, the present moment or *kairos* is a moment of crisis or decision. In it we choose the direction we wish to take, and in that choice, decide to create our particular future. Then, by performing the kinds of acts that will promote our choice and by avoiding those that will prevent its development, we create the future we selected. Thus, we cannot avoid the consequences of our present action. Ultimately, the meaning of what we do in the present is determined in the light of the end or future it will bring into existence. From the perspective of personal presence, the present moment, on the one hand, is an end in itself, a moment of living and sharing with others that is to be lived and enjoyed to the full. However, on the other hand, its precarious, fleeting nature is indicative of the fact that it is at the same time a means to a future end or goal. These reflections lead to the conclusion that personal presence is both the means and the end of life. The consequences of this conclusion can only be brought to light by analyzing the relationship between means and ends.

Personal Presence is the Means and End of Life

The means within any activity or process find their deepest meaning not in themselves, but in the

end they are used to achieve. This truth is fully
appreciated only when we come to see that means and
ends can never be radically separated, and that their
relationship is far more complex than a mere temporal
spread (the means preceding the end they bring into
existence). Nothing should be understood as a mere
means. Means live on in the end they help to achieve;
and at each step of the process, the desired end is
to some extent concretely realized in the means used
to achieve it. The end or culmination of a process is
never separate from the means by which it was attained, because the means and end become one and the
same thing. Let me provide two illustrations.

Theft is a means to becoming a millionaire, but
this means does not disappear the moment the robbery
is completed. It lives on, because the person has
become a millionaire thief. Cement, bricks, mortar
and other necessary materials are the means to build
a house. Once the cement foundation (means) has been
poured, the end (house) is already partially realized.
When the last shingle has been put on the roof, all
the means or materials used remain permanently, because the means and end have become the house. During
the building process, the meaning or purpose for which
specific materials (means) were united is not to be
found entirely in their use by itself, but in their
specific use in relation to the projected end, the
whole house.

These facts indicate that our old argument that
the end justifies the means is entirely false. Means
and ends cannot be evaluated separately. We cannot
commit ourselves to an end, unless we can also conscientiously commit ourselves to the means required to
achieve it, because means, and the consequences of
having chosen specific means, live on in the end.
Means are, as it were, an end being brought into existence. Thus, we can never understand or effectively
evaluate an end apart from the process by which we
brought it into existence and from which it can never
be totally separated.

It would be too repetitive to systematically spell
out all the ramifications of transposing these insights regarding means and ends to time and life understood in terms of personal presence. However, if
we are serious about creating a future that will be
truly personal out of the present, we shall have to
take the relationship between means and ends very

CREATING A FUTURE IN THE PRESENCE OF GOD   146

seriously. This will require shifting some of the
value we attribute to many current policies, possessions, attitudes and personal qualities to others
that are more conducive to fostering what is authentically personal. I shall restrict my comments here
to a few major shifts that are necessary if we are to
create a future in which we can live amicably in each
other's presence.

The world of things has gained such a strong hold
on our imaginations, desires, time and energy that
the world of people and that of the Spirit of God
tend to get edged out of our lives. We are masters at
creating, improving, possessing and enjoying things.
As much as these activities are necessary and good in
themselves, they remain part of the world of things
and utility. They are means, not the end of our existence. Therefore, we ought to ground their ultimate
justification on what they contribute to promoting
our peak experiences--knowing, loving and enjoying
each other. Yet, we too frequently subordinate the
personal to the material.

We place so much emphasis on activity and the
qualities that assure success in the world of things,
that we limit the capacity of our activities to promote the interpersonal life they are meant to create.
Because we tend to regard passivity (a willingness to
be acted upon or to suffer) as personal weakness, we
fail to achieve the necessary balance between it and
activity in our experience. It is in letting ourselves be acted upon that openness, listening and
receptivity are heightened. Therefore, when the passivity element in the dynamic that constitutes our
experience is not adequate, our greatest opportunities
for deepening personal relations, fostering personal
presence and developing community are partially lost,
and our experience itself is not as personally satisfying as it could be. The end achieved is more functional than personal, when it could be both.

The emphasis we place on success assures that we
concentrate on methods of interaction that promote
efficiency. We succeed, and are rewarded financially
or by promotion or some form of acclaim geared to
keep us in shape to keep at the job. The emphasis is
on developing such qualities as assertiveness, capacity for rational analysis and control, rather than on
the more personal qualities that promote presence. A
healthier mix or balance between qualities (means)

that produce success and those that foster presence would enrich our lives.

If we analyze our lives a step further, we see that we attribute value almost exclusively to the ends of our activities at the expense of the processes that lead to them. This separation of means and ends, with value being attached primarily to the external rewards we receive on achieving the ends, causes us to lose much of the satisfaction that flows from our activities themselves. We look at the processes involved in studying, working and performing so many other vital activities as mere drudgery to be gotten through as quickly and easily as possible. Having lost the personal fulfillment we should be getting from our experience of work itself, the further satisfaction of experiencing it as service to others and as building community is simply foreign to our consciousness. In brief, we do not allow the world of things the opportunity to enhance our interpersonal lives in ways it is most suited to do.

Furthermore, our possessiveness tends to make us see things immediately as good for us, rather than simply good in themselves. Possessiveness and greed limit our freedom and our capacity to move beyond what Maslow has been telling us for years is a way of perceiving the world in the narrow terms of our own deficiency needs. From the perspective of our motives to act, this is a relatively immature method of perception. It limits our capacity to transcend ourselves and to see things less selfishly and more objectively.[7] Thus, from what we have been saying, we need to shift some of the value we place on activity to that willingness to be acted upon that promotes personal growth, more consummatory experience, and more personal interaction. We also need to shift our vision from external rewards for our activities to the activities themselves. We should prize means, or the processes by which our goals are achieved, as much as our goals; and the meaning and value of our goals should always be determined in conjunction with the processes that make them possible.

It is also evident that we place too much value on situations in which one person's advantage can be gained only at the disadvantage of another. We constantly set up situations in which there are bound to be winners and losers, in spite of the fact that the goals and benefits we wish to achieve could be ob-

tained with much less competition. Competition is
essential to life. Without it the creativity and initiative necessary to build the future I am advocating
would simply be lacking. It is the excessive competition in our society that we must acknowledge and curb.

I think it is essential that institutions and
organizations in our society shift research funds to
study how to motivate us to commit ourselves to activities that promote our own advantage as well as
that of all the others involved. What is at stake
here is a shift from over-valuing keen competition to
valuing compassionate co-operation. It is my conten-
tion that this kind of shift is absolutely essential
if the arms race is to be halted and if labour and
management are going to switch from an adversary
stance to a co-operative posture in which honest give
and take in negotiations can be aimed at promoting
the good of all those involved.

Maslow pointed out the difference between the way
of knowing that operatives when we see our deficiency
needs and the way of knowing that enables us to get a
view of reality in its wholeness. Parallel to this,
he also distinguishes between those deficiency needs
and values that are primarily associated with utility,
and those values associated with the more integral
vision of more self-actualizing people. Honesty,
truth, beauty, goodness, uniqueness and wholeness
fall within this latter category of values. Some of
the needs associated with more integral vision and
its corresponding values are: self-esteem, dignity, a
feeling of worth, autonomy and respect for both oneself and others.8 These needs go beyond the realm
of utility, but fall within the range of pragmatic
consideration, because they are essential to the personal welfare of those involved and the common good
of our whole society. It seems essential, therefore,
that we attempt to fulfill needs and achieve values
on both levels at the same time.

For instance, it is certainly legitimate to ask
how labour could possibly think of either taking up
this more integral way of perceiving the reality it
must face or of diffusing its efforts by trying to
emphasize the latter set of values and personal needs
listed above, when so many workers still lack fundamental deficiency needs. Nevertheless, we ought not
to forget that we never progress in life to the point
where all our deficiency needs are satisfied, and

then move to the higher level of cognition, needs and
values being discussed here. Life and growth are never
that tidy, because deficiency needs are ongoing. If
we do not learn to reach beyond our deficiency needs,
motives and values at the same time as we satisfy
them, we run the risk of stifling ourselves at an
inadequate stage of development.

The economically restrictive situation of the
past few years has certainly helped to create what I
regard to be a genuine crisis and possible turning
point in labour negotiations. At times one fears
labour may lose some of the rights and advantages it
has worked so hard to achieve. The natural tendency
in this situation is to be aggressive in defending
fundamentals. Paradoxically, it may be the present
situation that forces the hand of both labour and
management to shift their vision and stance toward
each other. When either side looks at the situation
from the perspective of its own utilities, needs,
gains and values, it does not perceive the values of
the whole. Looking at realities in terms of utility
never leads to full perception. When each side funnels
its focus even further to concentrate on the consequences for itself alone, its perception is even more
restricted.

Asking representatives of the different levels of
labour and management in a company, as well as their
stock holders, to enter into an ongoing dialogue
geared at developing a statement evaluating the contribution their institution is making to society may
appear utopian. We tend to shy away from such value
laden assignments. However, sharing insights gained
from asking hard questions (a) about the real value
of the product or service the institution provides,
and (b) about the values operative in its policies
and decisions, will help everyone to enunciate the
institution's world view or philosophy. Every institution has such a view, but it is usually perceived,
and only partially articulated, by a few. It is this
kind of perception of the whole (a perception analogous to the loving knowledge that gives an integral
view of both strengths and weaknesses) that fosters
care, and so promotes commitment and a willingness to
make sacrifices for the good of the whole. Management
needs this kind of commitment in all its employees
and employees need to be given a broader vision of
the whole enterprise of which they are a part. The
opportunity to usher in a new era of dialogue between

labour and management may be available now, because
of the precarious nature of our present economic atmosphere. Achieving this kind of dialogue will involve
an extremely difficult shift from a vision and rheto-
ric that are adversarial to one of co-operation.
Undoubtedly, management and labour will make this
shift only if and when they are no longer willing to
suffer the consequences of their current way of being
present to each other.

We can only speak of promoting the common good,
as it is understood by Vatican II, when we work together to create a set of conditions that do whatever
is possible to favour the personal fulfillment of all
members of our society. The Council describes the
common good as "the sum of those conditions of social
life which allow social groups and their individual
members relatively thorough and ready access to their
own fulfillment."9 More and more, we are called to
take the responsibility of working together to determine and promote common goals that unite us to form a
genuine society. The ever tightening interdependence
among very disparate people in daily life is a relatively new phenomenon that requires shifts in attitudes and behaviour. We would do well, individually
and collectively, to devote more of our time and
energy to creating organizations that will foster the
common good by helping us to understand and cope with
this increased interdependence.

Let us move now from the world of work to the
very intimate experiences of being alone, experiencing
solitude and even loneliness. Through an examination
of these experiences, we shall recommend a few final
shifts in attitude and behaviour that are essential
if we are going to develop ourselves and personalize
time. Our compulsion to be busy, to be surrounded by
people, noise and activity, hinders our efforts to
personalize time and create a personalistic future,
because it prevents us from really being present to
ourselves. Part of the process of liberating ourselves
from this compulsion entails a shift from the attitude
that leads most of us to shun being alone toward a
greater appreciation of being alone, of solitude and
even a willingness to experience loneliness. This is
an extremely important shift, because these three
experiences enhance our self-knowledge to such an
extent that it is difficult to be genuinely present
to ourselves or to be honest and truthful with ourselves apart from them. Because they are such impor-

tant routes to self-understanding and presence to self, they are also indispensible means by which we come closer to each other.

Being alone is ordinarily no more than a state of being between personal encounters. The fact that we are not in the presence of others does not, of itself, indicate the way we experience such moments. Many people never give themselves the opportunity to really be alone with their own thoughts, imaginings and feelings. They blot these out by radio or television. Others fill such moments by planning ahead, evaluating the activities of their day or by a variety of other useful actions that consume the time productively. The behaviour of the first group is personally damaging; that of the second, as valuable as it is, prevents them from growth in genuine self-awareness, because it takes the place of more beneficial ways of being present to themselves. A much more beneficial alternative is to experience solitude or even loneliness.

Solitude is an extremely important way of personalizing our time, because it is a positive experience of being present to ourselves, coming in touch with the sources of creativity and voices that come from within, rather than from outside ourselves. In moments of solitude we overcome fear of discovering our true selves. Through the ascetic and spiritual experience of allowing our own diffuse imaginings, dreams and ideals to come to full bloom and acceptance, we activate internal powers that sensitize and cleanse us. Experiencing solitude is a privileged way of being present to ourselves. It helps to purge us of our false idols, distortions and deceptions, and so creates a new picture of reality as we reach out for the truth. Solitude enables us to come to life in our own way.10 It is a path to authenticity and self-renewal that provides a healthy balance to the over-socialized expressways on which we ordinarily find ourselves. Solitude is essential to creativity, because it brings us into contact with the depths from which our uniqueness emanates. In moments of inner silence (the absence of inner turmoil), facilitated by the beauty of nature, poetry, good music or art, we find ourselves, our neighbour and God. This occurs through an act of presence that is akin to experiencing the presence and hiddenness of God in contemplation.

Loneliness is an experience that is closely related, but distinct from solitude. It is more painful
than solitude, but except for those who have never
experienced real love, it is a positive, maturing
encounter with oneself. It is an intense experience
of being present to oneself that ought not to be
feared or avoided. Loneliness is a healthy testimony
to the fact that we are relational beings. The pain
of loneliness reveals that we are meant to love. Loneliness is an inevitable outcome of love, in the sense
that once love has been experienced, life without it
is loneliness. It is also a process through which we
grow to appreciate friendship and love, and so is an
experience through which new love becomes
possible.[11]

The kinds of experience that arouse feelings of
loneliness are rejection, misunderstanding, separation, divorce, failure, not living up to one's potential, guilt, tragedy, illness and death. These experiences flood in upon a us by suddenly threatening
or denying some aspect of our lives or vision of reality. At times, loneliness forces us to experience
the agony of living, suffering and dying in apparent
isolation. These are moments when, regardless of our
sincere intentions and efforts, we have to face our
limited capacity to be present to those we love. In
such experiences, when everything and everybody seems
to have been stripped away, we can only cling to our
faith in the presence of God. These moments of loneliness are immediate encounters with life at its extremes, moments when we feel cut off from the sources
of life and meaning and even from our very being.
This fact explains why loneliness is a very intense
experience of being beside and beyond ourselves.
Nevertheless, times of loneliness need not be negative, depersonalizing moments, because if we allow
the experience of loneliness to take its course, if
we live it intensely, it is not only a way of coming
back to ourselves, but a way of creating ourselves
anew.[12]

Much of our loneliness is due to our failure to
be honest, truthful and genuinely present to ourselves
and others. We feel the emptiness of our own existence
and our spiritual impotence when we are not faithful
to our values and identity. We make uneasy truces
with ourselves and others, and become estranged from
ourselves and those closest to us. We fail to stand
up for what we believe in difficult situations.

Through these failures, we deny our distinct selves
and fail to express our inner truth. The result is
loneliness.

We impact our loneliness when we try to cling to
ourselves at our present stage of development and
when we fail to realize our potential. We betray ourselves by placing all our faith in material success
and rewards. Loneliness has increased, rather than
decreased, with the accumulation of wealth in our
society. We have also allowed ourselves to fall prey
to numerous modern forms of slavery, such as constantly having to prove our self-worth and allowing ourselves to become workaholics. Loneliness is the lot
and the cry of the slave. Finally, we betray ourselves
even further, when we give in to the urge to escape
our moments of loneliness or to rescue others from
theirs. By doing so, we deprive ourselves of a normal
opportunity to be deeply present to ourselves in a
way that matures and liberates.

Loneliness has very extensive social consequences,
because it compels us to face our own personal guilt
in relationships and to acknowledge our need for intimacy and communion with those we have injured.
When we have the courage to stick with our loneliness,
we experience our need to be reconciled to ourselves
and others, to be forgiven, delivered and absolved
from our sins against our neighbours. Loneliness pre-
pares us for healing. This requires that our ways of
perceiving and relating with others be shifted to the
point where all other people are recognized and accepted as members of the same human family. In essence, therefore, loneliness is a painful, but positive, way of extending and deepening our humanity,
because it leads us to deeper commitment to people,
to lofty, personalistic ideals and to the concrete
practice of truth, wisdom and love.13

Loneliness can help us to appreciate the actu-
alizing capacity of love and the stultifying effect
of its absence. It can teach us that love is grounded,
not just in the immediacy of the present moment, but
in preparing for and sharing a common future. It can
help us to develop a healthy love of self based on
the truthfulness, honesty and other virtues we strive
to achieve, rather than on the number of our material
possessions or other illusory criteria. It reveals
the error of identifying ourselves in terms of our
possessions or the prestigious job we hold. Personal

identity is not achieved in terms of what we own, but
in terms of our values and our efforts to achieve
goals beyond our own self-interest. A search for
identity is a search for values.

Henri Nouwen points out that it is false to suppose that we grow closer to each other only when we
are in each other's presence, talking, playing or
working together. Solitude, silence, being alone and
being lonely are also indispensible experiences, if
we are to grow in our capactiy to be genuinely present to each other.14 The focus throughout this
book is on fostering personal presence. Paradoxical
as it may seem, we have shown that genuine presence
is fostered in part through the purifying, maturing
experience of the absence of our friends and loved
ones. The truth of the saying "absence makes the
heart grow fonder" is to be found, not on the senti-
mental, but on the much deeper level of the pain and
suffering their absence evokes. Moments of presence
derive their depth and reverence from the sensitivity
developed in moments of solitude and loneliness.
Therefore, it is a balance of loneliness and loving
that will enable us to personalize our time and strive
for an ever more personalistic future.

This discussion of solitude and loneliness can
provide us with a few final spin-off benefits by enabling us to appreciate certain personal qualities
and moral traits to which traditionally our North
American society has not given top priority. Among
the most obvious are empathy, openness, wide sympathy
and keen sensitivity. These are not the traits that
ordinarily come to the fore in the work mode of presence, because they don't guarantee success in the
short term. Nor are they ordinarily recognized as
serious moral virtues we have a genuine moral obligation to develop. I suggest a shift in our thinking
regarding these virtues. They are much more central
to the Christian life and the possibility of creating
a livable future than we ordinarily acknowledge.
Authenticity, a healthy balance of interests, concern
for wider, more universal goals and persistence in
the face of what is painful are also moral traits
crucial for fostering personal presence.

A deeper appreciation of the fact that all of us
are continually in process should help us to acknowledge that we are always incomplete and imperfect. It
should also help us to honestly accept our mistakes

and imperfections. This is a phenomenally liberating experience after which we no longer feel compelled to either justify or repeat our past. For instance, some parents are threatened when they recognize the serious mistakes they have or are still making in relating with their children. They are afraid to admit their errors, lest they lose authority and respect. Thus, there is a tendency for them to repeat the same behaviour, which is bound to make genuine presence between them and their children even more difficult. Acknowledging that we discover truth, values and our very selves in and through our experiences gives us added cause to back down in situations that need improving. We need to place more confidence in the truth of the insights our sensitivity and experience lead us to see. When this confidence is supported by the virtues of adaptability and detachment, it, in turn, liberates us to test the validity of our perceptions in our ongoing interactions.

One final insight into the meaning of human potentiality can be gained by bringing together our discussion of personal presence as the means and end of life and what we have said about loneliness as a creative means to presence. These discussions have consistently highlighted our relational nature. Too often we regard potentiality as limited to inherent capacities that enable us to develop beyond our present stage of realization. The acorn is said to possess the potential to become an oak tree; the child, to become a lawyer, honest citizen and loving parent. Without in any way denying inherent capacities within the acorn or the child, what sense does it make to speak of the potentiality of an acorn if it is not planted? It is only in potentiality to become an oak tree, in any meaningful sense, if it is grounded in reasonably rich soil where it gets enough light, food, moisture and space to grow. If it lacks any of these nurturing elements obtained through its ongoing interaction with its environment, it can only become a spindly, lopsided tree.

So too with a child. The real potentiality of a child cannot be adequately understood in terms of the physical, mental and emotional capacities inherent in it at birth. The child too has to be grounded in a loving, accepting, nourishing environment. If its parents do not provide it with their loving, supporting presence, like the oak tree, its potentiality is drastically reduced. The child, to some extent, will be emotionally, morally, spiritually and professionally handicapped; and without extraordinary interventions, will in turn be unable to provide the loving presence her/his children need to develop themselves fully as sensitive, loving people. Since genuine personal presence is so essential to developing human potential, and since our children are, in a real sense, our future, our most urgent challenge is to make the shifts and changes in public and personal attitudes and behaviour that are required if family life is to be restored from its state of rapid decline. Only by making sincere efforts to turn the tide in this area can we be assured that we are serious about creating a personalistic future.

Notes

1. For a more detailed interpretation of John Dewey's thought on pragmatism, with complete references to his works, see, *A Processive World View for Pragmatic Christians*, cited above, pp. 139-49.

2. Ibid., pp. 157-64.

3. Ibid., pp. 149-54.

4. *The Challenge of Peace: God's Promise and Our Response, Pastoral Statement of the U.S. Conference of Catholic Bishops* (Boston: Daughters of St. Paul Edition, 1983), parag. 68, p. 24, parag. 235, pp. 60-61.

5. Bok, pp. 28, 149-50.

6. Buber, "What is Common to All," *The Knowledge of Man*, p. 108.

7. Maslow, pp. 82-83.

8. Ibid., pp. 82-83, 202-03, 241.

9. Walter M. Abbott, ed., "Pastoral Constitution on the Church in the Modern World," *The Documents of Vatican II* (New York: The American Press, 1966), parag. 26, p. 225.

10. Moustakas, *Loneliness and Love*, pp. 40-42.

11. Eugene C. Kennedy, *Living with Loneliness* (Chicago: Thomas More Press, 1973), p. 95; Moustakas, *Loneliness and Love*, pp. 145-46.

12. Moustakas, *Loneliness and Love*, pp. 20-22, 45.

13. Moustakas, *Loneliness* (Englewood Cliffs, N.J.: Prentice-Hall, A Spectrum Book, 1961), pp. ix, 8, 11, 54-56, 102-03.

14. Henri J. M. Nouwen, *Clowning in Rome: Reflections on Solitude, Celibacy, Prayer, and Contemplation* (Garden City, N.Y.: Doubleday, An Image Book, 1979), pp. 13-14.

Chapter 7

FROM PRACTICAL ATHEISM TO DIVINE INDWELLING

Indications of Our Openness to God's Presence

A fundamental teaching of the Judaeo-Christian tradition is that God created all reality and continues to sustain it in existence. That is to say, God's presence is so essential to everything he has created that nothing can exist apart from it. Very early in our discussion of people as relational beings, we described creation as the act by which God brings the realities he creates into relationship with himself, and also, therefore, into relationship with all the other things he has created. Since our very existence is a gift of God, this relationship of dependence on him is the most fundamental of all our relationships. It is also the point from which we must start, if we are going to understand ourselves and establish our identity, both individually and collectively. If we deny or ignore this relationship, we miss something so essential to our self-understanding, that the other elements composing our person are seen out of their true context. A distorted picture of what it is to be a person results.

Although vast numbers of people in our society claim to have some connection with a religious tradition, it is not an exaggeration to say that the spiritual climate in which we live is that of practical atheism. In their day to day interactions, many people are unaware of or even consciously deny the presence and activity of God. They conceive of themselves as the exclusive cause of their accomplishments, and rarely, if ever, reflect on their radical dependence on God or on his presence maintaining them in existence and enabling them to accomplish the actions they perform. Because of indifference, practical convenience or simply an unwillingness to face ultimate questions, they live a life of practical atheism, while professing and occasionally even practising a religious faith. Without entering into a debate about moral responsibility or culpability for the practical atheism that permeates our society, it is consistent to affirm that it creates a widespread, but unconscious and indeliberate, dishonesty and untruthfulness that pervade our whole milieu. After all, if the Creator-creature relationship indicates that first and foremost we are dependent upon God, and therefore co-operators (co-creators) in our efforts to develop the world, we live a lie when we ignore this relationship in establishing our identity and when we approach the world as if we were solely and totally responsible for history.

There is some indication that our indifference toward the presence of God in our lives creates negative consequences, which we interpret and try to overcome by means other than opening ourselves to God. We find means that enable us to cope with many of these consequences with a fair amount of success. Nevertheless, the very presence of these consequences in our lives indicates that we are open to the transcendent and that we were created to live in the presence of God. Let us take a quick look at some of the indications in our lives that bear witness to Augustine's assertion that our hearts are meant for God and are restless until they find their fulfillment in his presence.

When, on the practical level, we ignore that we are creatures who share responsibility with God for making history and developing the universe, we place ourselves in a very difficult bind. On the one hand, we take upon ourselves total responsibility for making history. As the sole agents capable of creating a desirable future, we have an awesome responsibility that strains our powers and keeps us under constant pressure to make visible progress. On the other hand, we find ourselves confronted with a global situation and global crises in the face of which we stand powerless. Torn between our omnipotence and impotence, we suffer a strange form of schizophrenia that alienates us from ourselves and from each other. Our practical atheism tends to create, not only a false autonomy and identity, it also saddles us with an insupportable amount of responsibility and a loneliness about which we can do nothing. Our practical atheism, therefore,

is a serious cause of the individual and collective
identity crises that characterize our society. The
consequences of the alienation and identity crises in
our society, both in terms of attaining interior peace
and obtaining the co-operation essential to build a
world community, are devastating.

When we deny the existence of God, we create gods
for ourselves by absolutizing the particular. Among
the more honourable realities we absolutize are reason, science and technology. We have made fantastic
scientific and technological advances and gained physical control of even nuclear power. Yet, our control
of power by means of technology does not necessarily
give us control of our technology itself. Control is
relative to consequences and values. We do not have
control of our technology, because, in our confusion,
we have hardly begun to project and co-ordinate the
consequences and values we want it to produce in view
of achieving our most pressing goals. We still submit
our revolutionary, nuclear technology and energy to
such enterprises as the arms race and war. The result
of our attempts to absolutize the particular is a
very painful intellectual and moral confusion that,
among other things, continues to promote excessive
competition, excessive nationalism and the revival of
the old, biological law of the survival of the fittest. At the same time, this confusion hampers our
ability to achieve unity and universal brotherhood.

When we lose sight of the presence of God in our
lives, we also lose sight of the revealed truth that
we are created good by God. Too frequently the result
is the need to constantly prove our goodness and value
by achievements. Thus, as we have already seen, great
emphasis is placed on efficiency, achievement and
production and on conceiving of ourselves, above all
else, as workers or producers. As we have already
seen, a society that emphasizes production must also
consume what it produces in order to keep the economic
process in motion. Thus, we tend to get locked into
an over-achieve/over-consume cycle that is basically
dehumanizing. In the intellectual and moral confusion
mentioned above, we strive to limit population growth
in order to use less of the earth's resources, yet we
promote consumerism, apparently paying no heed to the
fact that increasing consumption has the same effect
as increasing population. Nor do we avert to the
fact that when we evaluate things exclusively in terms
of their utility, we rapidly exhaust them. Things

that exist simply for our use quickly bore us; we soon need something new. Thus, the depersonalizing spiral of production/consumption keeps us on another spiral of over-stimulation that leads to continual physical and mental strain.

What is true of things valued for their utility alone is equally true of people. They too are soon consumed and discarded. It is not difficult to understand why the playgirl/playboy philosophy of use and enjoy without becoming emotionally involved or committed leaves so many people confused and alienated from themselves and each other. This approach is an unconscious use of sex to create an identity. Sex retains the form of a highly organized game with its own rules dictating what is cool from what is tacky. Yet, it is reduced to a form of work, because the partners come to each other as traders, makers and consumers, who are too often anxious about their performance and concerned with how well they are achieving their primary goal--maximum pleasure.

Although sex is said to be the essence of fun, its playful and ecstatic dimensions are lost. The partners are led to center on themselves, their own individual performance, feelings and technique. In fact, the playgirl/playboy is the extreme reaction to the Puritan; both fear the total reality of sex. Whereas the playgirl/playboy accepts the intense pleasure and nervous excitement, but fears the emotional attachment and commitment involved in authentic sexual love, the Puritan fears the former and accepts the latter. Both these extreme approaches deny that sexual intimacy is a privileged expression of love that promotes personal presence in its richest form.

The playgirl/playboy philosophy implies that we can reduce sexual love and intimacy to a functional relationship, where use and pleasure predominate, without experiencing any detrimental consequences. Yet, the widespread search for casual sexual partners, with little more meaning than to get each other through the night, has led to a sexual inflation in which many experience an almost compulsive need for more and more sex, yet receive less and less satisfaction from it. This lack of adequate satisfaction, when sex is reduced to trading and consumption, is an intimation of its real capacity to be an authentically ecstatic experience that takes the partners beyond themselves to find themselves loved, enriched and

affirmed in and by each other. Scripture presents
sexual love as an image of the love of Christ for his
people. It indicates that sex is at one and the same
time a secular reality and sacred mystery that can
speak to the partners of the love and presence of God
to them in and through their intimate personal presence to each other. The evident limitations of the
playgirl/playboy approach implies that there is more
to human sex than is commonly acknowledged today, and
challenges us to search once again to experience the
truth of the richer understanding of sex offered in
the scriptures.

Another area of life that suffers from our compulsion to make history all by ourselves is leisure.
Our proclivity to see ourselves as achievers is one
of the major factors that has contributed to losing
sight of the real meaning and reality of leisure. We
define leisure as time off from work or think of it
solely in terms of the leisure activities we use to
consume our free time. Many do not enjoy their work,
so they pursue leisure activities vigorously in the
attempt to extract from them as much pleasure and
satisfaction as possible. In a sense, leisure is
thought of as an extended coffee break. It is either
a reward for work already accomplished or a means of
re-creating ourselves to go back to work more efficiently. This approach defines leisure in terms of
work and circumscribes it within the world of work.
In reality, leisure is so different from this that
when we try to reduce it to these dimensions it eludes
us completely.

In order to gain further insight into how and why
leisure has been lost, let us look to the loss of
contemplation and contemplative knowledge in our
society. Contemplation has been variously defined as
a simple, unimpeded, penetrating gaze on Truth; a
long loving look at the real, and freedom from the
necessity of being occupied, interiorly and/or exteri-
orly. Contemplation is not simply an activity; it is
an attitude and a whole way of being and living.
Contemplative knowledge is loving knowledge that
grasps the reality known in its wholeness and basks
in it as it is, rather than desiring to change it.

Leisure is primarily a contemplative attitude, an
attitude of contemplative celebration. It is an attitude that draws its vitality from affirmation, and so
is only possible when we affirm ourselves, the uni-

verse and our place within the whole. In leisure we affirm that our own being, life and the world are good. Leisure is only possible for us, as individuals and as a society, when we know, love and are at peace with ourselves.[1]

Since we affirm particular realities by celebrating them, the essence of leisure is in celebration; and leisure and celebration find their ultimate meaning and justification on the same basis, divine worship. In leisure we affirm and celebrate life and the universe. The most intense affirmation of life and the world is the praise of God for having given us these gifts. The most affirmative and festive of all celebrations is divine worship.[2] Having lost the experience of this reality, it is not surprising that we have become confused about the meaning of leisure.

Leisure and leisure activities are concerned with things done for their own sake. We have lost respect for pure play and games; they are for children, not adults. We concentrate on recreational activities that have social value and on competitive sports and athletics which are disciplined, rule-regulated, competitive activities more akin to work than play. We mistrust what is effortless and what is given to us. In over-emphasizing the importance of work, even if we get little satisfaction from it, we attribute a functional benefit to leisure; its purpose is to enable us to become better workers. In reality, it enables us to become more human--better people.

We tend to envy the unemployed, because they have all that leisure. In fact, however, being without work reduces their self-esteem, alienates them from themselves, and makes real leisure impossible for them. The inability of either the unemployed or even those who are lazy or slothful to maintain inner calm or silence, and/or to acquiesce in their own being, assures that their free time is more of a burden than an opportunity for leisure. The loss of genuine leisure, and the accompanying pervasive, ill-defined anxiety, tension and sleeplessness so common among us, are other indications of our need to transcend our world of utility and to experience the peace associated with experiencing the presence of God.

We have already seen that contemplation and solitude are means of enabling us to be present to our-

selves, to the beauty and truth of nature and to each
other in a very penetrating manner. These activities
also have the capacity to bring us into the presence
of God, and there is evidence today that at least
unconsciously we hunger for his presence. In recent
years, as we have become more and more cut off from
our own religious roots, we have sought experience of
the transcendent in new philosophies, the occult,
drugs and other experiences that might enable us to
go beyond our own limitations.

Many have overcome the lack of meaning, the alienation and the feeling of being abandoned by active
involvement in moral and social movements aimed at
removing poverty, reducing oppression, overcoming
racism and protesting the arms race. Yet, many have
found that as much as these activities help, they do
not remove their poverty and abandonment of spirit,
nor do they satisfy all the longings of their hearts.
Contemplative prayer, through which we take a long,
relaxed, but penetrating gaze on Truth or God, opens
us to his presence in an in-depth manner not available
through other experiences. The experience of God's
presence through contemplative prayer has the effect
of satisfying our deep, inner longing for peace, integrity and meaning.[3]

We have also seen the role of solitude in enabling
us to be present to ourselves and to nature in an
exceptionally creative fashion. It brings us into
contact with the deep, creative resources in our own
being and the inner beauty and harmony of nature. It
is not surprising, therefore, that solitude has the
capacity to open us to experience the Creator in and
through his creation. By revealing our restlessness,
compulsiveness, fear, anger and need to make quick
contact lest life simply pass us by, solitude unmasks
our false image of ourselves. In doing so, it opens
us to the depth dimensions of our own being, where we
get at least periodic glimpses of the presence of God
within ourselves. Solitude, like contemplation, enables us to experience ourselves as open, receptive
and vulnerable in the presence of the God within, a
God who wants to give himself and, in return, be loved
by us. By stripping away our false identity and our
mistaken concept of God as a being who is out there
rather than within, solitude creates a space within
each of us for the presence of others. Through encounter with the God within us, we experience a new
capacity for solidarity with other people.[4]

Undoubtedly, one of the most painful intimations that we are open to a transcendent/immanent God is a deep, inner loneliness for which there seems to be no remedy. In an extremely insightful work, *The Inner Loneliness*, Sebastian Moore points out that ordinary experiences of living compel us to feel our fundamental incompleteness, mortality and dependence, but do not provide the meaning of these realities. There is a genuine sense in which individual people experience and appreciate their own wholeness or integrity, while at the same time realizing that they are relational and in need of participating in the lives of others in order to become themselves. This tension is concretized in our sexual identity, through which we experience a certain incompleteness expressed as a need for sexual intimacy and union with another.

The natural conclusion for both female and male alike is that it is only with a partner of the opposite sex that s/he will know her/himself as woman or man. Yet, experience teaches that both women and men are constituted as sexual beings by a nature that is powerless of itself to reveal to them the mystery of their sexual identity. At the heart of everyone is a loneliness that every other person experiences, so that no one is able to relieve this loneliness in another. In brief, there is an element of mystery about our personal, sexual identity that neither nature nor intimacy can reveal to us. We have to search within ourselves individually the meaning of our sexual identity, and so everyone experiences a deep inner loneliness.

On two other levels, we are led to the same experience of inner loneliness, because, once again, nature can tell us only so much about ourselves and then goes silent. Through suffering over the death of our loved ones and by experiencing our own process of aging, the world tells us that we are mortal. On another level, the earth itself also reminds us of our radical dependence, not only on other people, but on our environment. In the face of our incompleteness, mortality and dependence, we are given no adequate answer to our own inner, personal meaning. This silence, or lack of meaning, is the condition of a loneliness that impels us to search within ourselves for understanding.[5]

It is a sense of our own uniqueness that impels us to seek union with another. However, paradoxically, this very uniqueness, that moves us to intimacy, places limitations on the intensity of the union that can be achieved. No other person can penetrate me to the point of knowing me as I know myself, nor can anyone touch me as I feel myself. Therefore, no one can be present to me as I am present to myself. Yet, I need and want to be totally understood. In my seemingly insatiable need for love, I want a partner whose very "to be" is "to be for me." In other words, we want others to know our hearts and to let us know theirs as only God is capable of doing. We want our marriage partner to be God for us and to allow us to be God for her/him. To be well, in the fully human sense, is to be for, to exist for the other. In our friendships and marriages, we want to penetrate and enter each other totally, and through the depths of this union, to be led forth into the whole ecstacy of existence. We have already seen that, according to the Christian understanding, sexual union is meant to be ecstatic; but people, and their capacity for friendship and union, are finite. God alone is capable of being absolutely intimate (being for us) and absolutely other (being himself). He alone is capable of fulfilling our desires and of satisfying our infinite need for personal presence. Thus, God alone can satisfy the inner longing and loneliness at the core of our being.[6]

The purpose of Christ's resurrection is to enable him to continue to be present to us, to be God-with-us. One of the most effective, modern christological titles given Jesus is the-man-for-others. We do not have an unlimited capacity to be for others, by virtue of the limits of our own human nature. However, this capacity is available to us, if we open ourselves to participate in the life of the risen Christ, whose very nature and purpose is to be for us. It appears, therefore, that the only way to adequately overcome the deepest, inner loneliness we experience is by opening ourselves to God.

Moore indicates that the way to obtain a very deep understanding of our sexuality is in terms of this inner loneliness, which is a craving for God. What he says is very important, in my estimation, for understanding the beauty, as well as the difficulty, of achieving personal presence through sexual union. In fact, I have avoided an in-depth analysis of personal presence through sexual intimacy up to this point in order to be able to bring together what I described above as its secular reality and sacred mystery.

The Genesis creation myth is not simply a story of the complementarity of the sexes and of God as Creator. It is the story of woman, man and God. First God creates a human, Adam; but seeing that Adam is lonely, differentiates the human into man (ish) and woman (isha). They are to find their meaning in each other, but only provided they find the meaning of their respective sexual differentiation in God. Both the female and male are meant to find God within themselves. Thus, they are to find in their sexual partner, not merely a being to complete them on the level of functional complementarity, but a person open to and in the presence of the infinite.[7]

In the Genesis myth of the fall, Adam and Eve break with their companion, God. This action is the beginning of the deep, inner, cosmic loneliness of mankind. We are told that the immediate effect experienced by Adam and Eve on breaking with God is a discomfort with their bodies in each other's presence. They see they are naked, and so make loinclothes for themselves out of fig leaves. Then they tell God they are hiding from him because of their nakedness. The Christian tradition states that the immediate consequence of this break with God is disorder in the passions, which in sexual matters is lust. Moore indicates that the biblical text clearly states that the immediate consequence is shame. That is to say, the immediate effect of cutting ourselves off from God is being ill at ease with our sexuality. It is no longer a friend, but a threat; and because we do not befriend it, it is out of control. This is the meaning of lust. From this perspective shame precedes and generates lust; lust does not generate shame.[8]

Our deepest loneliness is experienced when we do not find an answer to the question "who am I?". Yet neither our bodies nor our sexual partner can answer this question adequately for us. We are ill at ease with our sexuality; we fear it and associate it with loss of control. Thus, there is a tension within us between our sexual desire and our need to control it. From this tension springs the difficulty in uniting friendship and passion. As we have seen, the Puritan, in accepting friendship and rejecting passion, and the playgirl/playboy, in accepting passion and rejecting committed friendship, have tried to dissolve this tension by simply rejecting one or other of the realities involved.

The person who cannot befriend her/his sexuality has difficulty giving it in a friendly way to a partner. Thus, tension in marriages arises when the same easy give and take that characterizes the partners' ordinary communication seems to be replaced by a different dynamic in moments of passion. Their love of self appears to be or is disconnected from their act of giving themselves in intercourse. Yet, they are constituted so that their love of self and gift of self are one, the former coming to full bloom in the latter. The radical unity between the way pleasure works and the way giving of self works means that pleasure achieves its full intensity only in the gift of self; and the gift of self loses all traces of inhibition, moralism and condescension in pleasure.[9] This integration of love of self and gift of self does not come easily. However, the realization that it is achievable, and that sexual intimacy is a way of encountering the presence of God in and through union with one's spouse, are indications of the extent to which sexual love is a privileged experience of personal presence in its richest sense.

We have been talking about a deep, personal loneliness that all of us feel in some way or other. Some experience it only indirectly as a pervasive restlessness and discontent that they cannot pinpoint. Others, realizing it is loneliness, experience it as an insatiable, inner longing; but do not recognize it as a hunger for the divine. Finally, others recognize, through faith, that this otherwise insatiable loneliness is due to the openness and longing in all human beings for the infinite, the divine.[10] These people experience the genuinely religious dimension of facing themselves in loneliness. This tends to remove a tremendous burden from their marriages and even from other friendships, because now they can allow their spouse and friends to be finite. They no longer expect them to satisfy all their aspirations and needs for intimacy. When our inner loneliness opens us to the divine, it not only assists our marriage relationsips, but helps us to discover what binds us together to form community. Although there are no easy answers and no solution to this loneliness, it is a catalyst that moves us to take up the arduous challenge of attempting to live in the presence of God. Since this is impossible without ac-

cepting the sufferings involved in developing friendships and community, this loneliness ultimately becomes a factor in helping us to work out our
salvation.

So far, in this chapter, we have looked at a number of indications that intimate that people are
called to live in the presence of the divine. These
are neither proofs of the existence of God nor proofs
that we cannot live without him. Those who choose to
live their lives without God, or with an absolute of
their own making, experience certain consequences.
So do those who choose in faith to accept the existence of a personal God and try to live in his presence. I have certainly implied that, looked at from
the perspective of achieving one's self-realization
in terms of enriched personal presence, there are
unfavourable consequences of not opening oneself to
the presence of God. It would be abhorrent, however,
to imply that God is our problem solver or that we
have a right to try to reduce God to that level.
That is a most unworthy and inauthentic form of religious response.

Striving to live our lives in the presence of God
is not going to solve our problems. People of faith
will willingly admit that in one sense the presence
of God in their lives changes nothing. All the old
problems and situations remain and still have to be
coped with from day to day. Nevertheless, these same
people will also admit that everything is changed by
the presence of God in their lives in ways that are
hard to spell out analytically. I shall attempt to
give some theological explanation for this radical
change, when I discuss the indwelling of the Holy
Spirit. At the moment, let me sum up my thought here
by showing how we place limits on ourselves that cause
us to suffer, in spite of the fact that our spirits
aspire to live without limits.

Everyone acknowledges that the mature person is
one who tries to achieve wholeness in life and the
greatest depth and breadth attainable in her/his overall view of reality. Yet, we have already seen that
we tend to place restrictions on our knowledge; we
reject the loving, contemplative knowledge that we
have seen is so valuable in knowing people holis-
tically. We also tend to regard anything that transcends sense experience as anti-rational, and therefore invalid. The rejection of assumptions made on

the basis of faith in revelation is also a real limitation to thought, because rejecting certain assumptions entails rejecting whole areas of thought and
possibilities that flow from them. On the other hand,
the use of such assumptions is valid on the grounds
that none of our basic assumptions can be proven right
or wrong prior to inquiry. Their truth has to be
demonstrated by observing the coherence of their consequences with knowledge attained from other sources.

Knowledge acquired on the basis of revelation can
be put to a type of pragmatic test. One can inquire
into the pragmatic meaning of any religious statement
in such a way as to show its fittingness, without
attempting to give an empirical proof for it. The
practical atheist tends to reject anything that transcends sense experience, and seeks complete openness
to truth by an initial rejection of religious assumptions. The believer seeks the same openness by accepting the possible validity of religious assumptions, and then demonstrates their fittingness in
terms of their coherence with thought arising from
other sources. The latter appears to be the more
liberal, open approach.

There is a genuine interest today in religious
and theological discourse by which we grapple with
and attempt to grasp an intellectual understanding of
religious realities. Many people wonder why this
approach does not automatically lead them to religious
faith. They are unaware that there is another whole
approach to God which, although not opposed to grasping facts about him, is primarily an opening of one's
person in readiness to be grasped by him. There is a
parallel here between these approaches to knowing God
and the biblical distinction between knowledge and
ignorance of God. Neither knowing or being ignorant
of God, in the biblical sense, is limited to an intellectual knowledge of facts about God. To know God is
to make a choice to allow him to be present and active
in our lives here and now. To be ignorant of God is
not to know and accept his presence and activity in
our lives in a very concrete way.

Faith forces us to break the boundaries we tend
to place on rational discourse, when it reaches the
frontiers of sense experience. Going beyond these
boundaries, however, does not destroy our human wisdom, but extends and enriches it by placing it in a
larger context. In this same paradoxical way, the

conflict between grace (the effect of opening ourselves to the gift of God's light, power and love)
and pride (cutting ourselves off from these by in-
sisting on our own absolute autonomy) confirms the
paradoxical wisdom or logic of the cross by which we
symbolize the passover from our own, absolutized autonomy into life in God. It is the conviction of
believers that in spite of our fantastic accumulation
of truth about the world, life and ourselves, the
real possibility of an enriched, expanded vision made
possible on the basis of accepting biblical revelation
is a constant challenge. We must ask ourselves if we
strive for an ever increased knowledge or for genuine
wisdom as well.

The functional culture in which we live drastically limits our capacity to open ourselves to God and
religion. As we have seen, functionaries take a pro-
ject-like approach to life, one in which aggression
and activity immediately come to the fore. We see
ourselves first and foremost as doers, not as receiv-
ers. We tend to mistrust gifts, because they are not
the fruit of our own efforts. However, grace, prayer
and religion are gifts. God takes the initiative in
revealing himself and giving us a share in his life.
It is not surprising, therefore, that the religious
dimension gets squeezed out of our lives, in spite of
the fact that it is by definition the depth dimension
of life. This, of course, is a great tragedy, because
committing ourselves to difficult tasks, like fostering world community, is impossible without insight
into our ultimate meaning. So too, human love tends
to go out to the particular; divine love is universal.
It is very difficult for us to develop the universal
love required for world community without the assistance of the love of the Holy Spirit. The human mind,
as well, often becomes negative and sees situations
in a light that divides rather than unites, when it
is not enlightened by the wisdom of the Spirit.

In the light of what has been said, it.seems to
me that there is a genuine reasonableness to the biblical vision of the world, created and sustained by
God, marred by our sin, but redeemed in Christ, so
that the whole may achieve its fulfillment in the
fullness of God's presence or kingdom. The teaching
that the purpose of the whole creative-redemptive
process is our happiness also becomes a challenge to
take seriously God's charge to "be still, and know
that I am God" (Ps. 46:10). It is an invitation to

lay aside our anxiety and our need for constant stimu-
lation, activity and satisfaction. These distractions
not only obstruct God's presence in all of us, they
make it very difficult for those searching for God to
find him in those who profess to live by his life.
Nouwen points out that the word person comes from
personare which means "sound through." It is the
role, especially of believers, to live as people who
sound through to others the presence of God.11 Since
we cannot reflect to others what is not a genuine part
of ourselves, we find here a call to accept the trials
and sufferings that are part and parcel of opening
ourselves to universal brotherhood and to the presence
of God.

Life in God's Presence is Fulfilled in Eternity

If we are going to commit ourselves to the Judaeo-
Christian belief that God not only creates, but also
sustains created reality in existence, we have to
strive for further insight into the most fundamental
way God is present to us. We know (a) that we are not
the cause of our own existence, (b) that we cannot
maintain ourselves in existence through our own delib-
eration alone, and, (c) that the most fundamental
biological functions that sustain us operate automatically and beyond our conscious control. Faith's answer to this mysterious aspect of life is that God's
presence maintains us in existence. It is impossible
to comprehend how this is done, but by analogy we can
gain a few helpful insights that may make the very
thought of his presence less difficult for us. We
shall start by analyzing an example of local motion.

Let us imagine a book at rest on a smooth table.
It must be touched by my hand, if it is to be moved
across that surface. There are four inseparable and
simultaneous elements involved in this motion: the
book, which of itself is passive, but capable of receiving motion from me; my hand, which is an active
source of motion; the touch of my hand to the book,
which is the specific mode of contact or presence
essential to produce the motion in question; and a
smooth surface, which provides a milieu compatible
with the desired motion. Without any one of these
elements, no motion can occur. Unlike the book, even
when I am unconscious, I am always in motion. That
is to say, my vital activities are always operating.

I did not put them in motion, nor do I consciously keep them operating. I am being sustained in motion by an active principle, which is the touch or presence of God. I am also in an environment that supports my life and activity. Thus, all four of the elements discussed in the example above are present, inseparable and interacting simultaneously, as God maintains me in my environment.

This example provides some insight into God's presence to us, but it is not really adequate, because God is present to his creation as an internal activator, not an external pusher. Thus, we shall look at another analogous illustration that will take us one step further. An electric motor can produce no motion unless it is activated by electricity and attached to a specific piece of machinery such as a pump. Once it is activated by electricity, the motion it produces is not only different from the electricity, but also varies in accord with the type of machine in operation. Once again, the four elements discussed above are present. The motor and its machine are capable of receiving the electricity; the electricity is the activating principle; as long as the switch is on, the electricity enters or is present to the motor activating it from within; while the motor and machine to which it is attached are in working condition, they perform an activity in accord with the nature of that specific machine.

This illustration gives us a little closer glimpse at the way God is present in his creation. The mere fact that a thing or person is in motion (in existence) indicates that God is interiorly present to or touching it. God's presence enables the thing or person to exist and perform its proper activities. Created reality is plugged into God, if you like, on this basic level of existence. This unconscious, unobservable presence of God to all things sustains them in being. The presence of God to all created reality also brings us face to face with the mystery of his transcendence and immanence.

God is not a particular being like you and I; he is Being. Nor is he corporeal. Because he is spiritual and infinite, he cannot body forth his presence to his creation in the way we are present to each other through our bodies. His presence is, of necessity, a hidden presence. Because he is infinite and pure spirit, he is absolutely transcendent. There-

fore, there are no limits to his capacity to be present to reality. At the same time, his presence,
being spiritual rather than corporeal, is an interior
presence. He is immanent within created reality. In
fact, God's sustaining presence on this fundamental
level of being is so interior that it is at the core
of all reality, where we cannot get a direct experience of it. It is also so extensive that experience
of it cannot be grasped on the level of observation.
In brief, the sustaining presence of God to all reality is so interior and so extensive that it is impossible to be aware of it on the level of observation
at all. His absolute transcendence and immanence are
so intimately related that he has the capacity to be
invisibly present to all reality as source, sustaining
foundation and end. It is this divine concourse on
the ontological level that is discussed in Acts 17:25,
where we read that "it is he who gives everything-
including life and breath--to everyone." The divine
presence is discussed again three verses later, where
it states that "in fact he is not far from any of us,
since it is in him that we live, and move, and exist,"
(Acts 17:28).

There is another mode of divine presence to people
by which God gives them a share in his very life and
enables their actions to be redemptive. I shall discuss it shortly. However, before moving to the reality of grace, I shall discuss the statement in John
15:5 that "cut off from me you can do nothing" as an
expression of divine concourse on the ontological
level. This is a negative statement, which we tend
to translate into positive terms. We think that if
we can do nothing without him, with him we can do
everything. This understanding is inaccurate. The
scripture is telling us that we do everything we do
with God. He is present to us enabling us to act,
whether we choose to perform virtuous or vicious acts.
Everything we can do is possible because of his presence to us. This point is made more clear in an al-
ternate translation of John 15:5, which reads "without
me" in place of "cut off from me."

On the most fundamental level, therefore, we don't
have to struggle to find God in our lives. We can be
absolutely assured that God is present and active in
us, simply because we exist. He is present as an
interior activator. Our tendency to misinterpret
John 15:5, when we translate it into positive terms,
has had very unfortunate consequences for our under-

standing of his presence in us. Once we begin to
believe that with him we can do all things, we start
to look for signs of either his presence or apparent
absence in us from the effects of our actions. If we
succeed in our affairs, if we perform acts that we
regard to be morally approvable, we feel assured of
God's presence assisting us. However, if the tide
turns against us and we fail, or if we act in a manner
that is reprehensible, we feel that somehow or other
we have been abandoned by God, that he is not present
to us.

This feeling of being abandoned by him often leads
us to an anxious struggle to bring ourselves into his
presence. We forget that God is not our concept of
him and that we cannot come into his presence by
striving to come in contact with our own idea of him.
We come in contact with God first by realizing he is
touching us, by realizing he is the source of all
movement in us. Therefore, the way to be in his presence is to look for him as the source of our movement,
not in the effects of our actions. These are far too
illusive and deceptive to act as a register of God's
presence to us.

The divine concourse we have been discussing assures God's presence and is the ontological foundation
for the gift of grace. Grace is God's offer of a
share in his life available to us through the gift of
the indwelling Holy Spirit. This is a more personal
mode of divine presence than the divine concourse.
It is possible, because, as spiritual beings, we have
the capacity to receive a share in his life and to
enter into a personal relationship with him. As indicated in one of the examples above, that which is
received is received according to the mode of the
recipient. Because we are free, intelligent beings,
God will not force us into a relationship with him.
Therefore, he can only be present to us in this personal manner to the extent that we are open and willing to receive him into our lives.

So far we have seen two distinct, but intimately
related, modes of divine presence to people: physical
concourse, which we share with the rest of creation;
and grace, which brings us into the divine life on a
conscious, personal level. In both these modes, God
is present as activator. Through grace we receive a
share in God's wisdom and love, and so have a power
or capacity to perform actions that are beyond our

own unaided, human powers. The ideal, therefore, is
to be open to God on both the ontological and spiritual levels, so that he can activate us in everything
we are and do. This creates a unity of being and mind
within us.

God is our activator. He is not only the source
of our lives, but when we consciously live in union
with him, he activates even our slightest movements.
He gives to us out of love and calls us to use what
we have been given to respond in love to the people
and situations in and through whom he is present to
us every moment of our lives. He dwells within us
spiritually and, through that presence, moves us to
respond to him in those we encounter. "I tell you
solemnly, in so far as you did this to one of the
least of these brothers of mine, you did it to me"
(Mt. 25:40).

After treating the Lord's work and prayer, Luke
moves on to discuss the Lord's power (11: 14-36).
Jesus insists that he has power to preach the good
news, to heal and to overcome the forces of evil,
because he possesses the power of the Spirit. Those
who think his power to cast out evil spirits comes
from the evil one are told that they themselves are
succumbing to evil. Even those who have been cured
of an unclean spirit are warned that they have no
guarantee of always remaining free in the future,
unless they receive the power of the Spirit to do
so. In response to Jesus' teaching, a woman in the
crowd exclaims, "'Happy the womb that bore you and
the breasts you sucked!" But he replied, "Still
happier those who hear the word of God and keep it!'"
(Lk. 11:27-28). Biblical scholars are quick to point
out that Jesus uses her interjection to teach that it
is not enough to declare the human origin of his
life to be blessed. Mary is blessed, because she is
the supreme example of a person of faith, a receptive
hearer, who pondered the word of God and made her
whole life a response to it. Jesus sets forth the
condition or sign of holiness--hearing the word of
God and keeping it. This activity exceeds the purely
human, and is possible only when we open ourselves to
an influx of divine power, and then remain in or cling
to that power.

What biblical exegetes do not do is analyze the
symbolic language of these two verses. The words
appear to have been deliberately chosen to highlight

the redemptive process: God always takes the initiative in giving; we receive from him first, and then
use his gift to respond to him in and through our
neighbour. The womb is a symbol of receptivity.
After it has received and been made fruitful, the
breasts are also fructified, so that they become a
symbol of life-giving activity. In a parallel
fashion, fearing is a sense by which we receive. In
this respect, its activity is parallel to that of the
womb. After our ears have received the word of God,
and we have been fructified by it, we are able to
live it. Then, and only then, are we able to perform
life-giving activities with our entire bodies. In
the case of human generation, what is received is
human and the outcome is human; receiving the word of
God in faith is a divine gift, and the outcome is
beyond unaided, human power. Once we have received
the grace of God, his life transforms us from within.
We are redeemed and all our actions are redemptive.
Everything we do flows primarily from God as its
source. It appears to me that we have here, in symbolic language, a paradigm for the fundamental action
of redemption (first receive from God and then respond), that ought not to be overlooked.

When we do not acknowledge God's presence nor
allow his activating power to be operative in our
lives, everything we do comes from ourselves. If we
act without first having received from the Lord, our
action, being purely human, lacks the redemptive power
of the Spirit. Mentally and spiritually we become
both activator and activated, which fragments and
divides us within ourselves. This is especially true
in time of temptation, when we are torn interiorly by
a desire to do that which we do not judge to be right.
If we do not open ourselves entirely to the working
of the Spirit, enabling him to activate our whole
being, that part of us that is striving for the good
attempts to activate that part that is attracted to
the evil at hand. We are a house already divided,
and we soon fall.

We deceive and enslave ourselves terribly, when
we keep looking for the presence of God in the effects
of our actions and when we keep clinging to our own
experience and knowledge of God, as if these were
God. These are created realities. Not even our desire for union with God is what enables us to achieve
that union. When we speak from ourselves as from the
source of our wisdom, we continue to cling to our own

lives and to what is not God. This is to remain
daughters and sons of iniquity. "Anyone who loves
his life loses it; anyone who hates his life in this
world will keep it for the eternal life" (Jn. 12:25).
When, in faith, we yield to the working of the Spirit
in us, we stop our own excessive pushing and striving
and cling to the source. By doing so, we give the
Spirit the opportunity to feed and fill us on an ongoing basis. Thus, we can receive what we say and do
from him as we say and do it.

On the other hand, when we do not let God be God,
by acknowledging our dependence upon him, we try to
be God ourselves. We are told that "'If you make my
word your home you will indeed be my disciples, you
will learn the truth and the truth will make you
free'" (Jn. 8:31-32). The truth that liberates us
is the fact that we are not the source of our own
being nor solely responsible for history. Our propen-
sity to absolutize our autonomy and our strengths has
made us compete with God for complete control of our
lives and the universe. Emphasis on one's strength
always makes one competitive; acknowledging dependence
and weakness creates unity. Therefore, admitting our
weakness and need for divine grace will go a long way
in uniting us with our neighbour and liberating us to
work together to build an open-ended future in which
all can participate as equals.

The problem of open-enedness is extremely crucial, because, as we have already seen, ultimately,
we determine the meaning of our actions in the light
of their ends. We refuse to take a step to pursue a
road or course of action that is not open-ended, and
therefore meaningful to us. An act is open-ended if
it fosters life, not if it leads to death; and what
is true of individual acts is also true of life itself. Both our individual acts and our lives as a
whole lose much of their meaning, if our lives simply
terminate in death--life itself would not be open-
ended under such circumstances. There would be no
absolute value to our person, and our works would
appear to be more important than we are ourselves.
The impersonality of such a situatioń, however, would
limit the psychological motivation we need to enable
us to face the risks and hardships inherent in the
performance of our daily work and the suffering involved in entering into lasting personal relationships.

If our personal relationships and acts are completely terminated by death, neither we nor our acts can transcend time. However, we know that an action is limited to neither the immediate moment of time in which we perform it nor to its temporal consequences; it is radically transcendent. We conceive of and experience a need to enter into personal relations and to perform acts that can come to a final consummation, and not be prematurely frustrated by ending in a mere stoppage like death. For us to have conceived this possibility and experienced this need, and then not be able to achieve it, would be the most frustrating and psychologically destructive experience possible. It would cripple our motivation and commitment to each other and to building community. It would stifle our whole spiritual lives. We need a universe that is personal and personalizing, one that fosters our ongoing personal development. But, we need to know that our works have some lasting value and that our efforts to build a world community are in some way related to our own, ultimate fulfillment. We also need the possibility of a final self-realization that fulfills our deepest aspirations, if we are to retain the vitality of spirit required for perseverance and commitment now.

The most satisfying form of self-realization we can imagine necessarily involves the full exercise of our most characteristic actions. These are our acts of knowing, loving and enjoying each other, acts which we have seen are acts of personal presence in its fullest sense. Ultimately, then, the only satisfactory end for our present processes of knowing and loving must be unending knowing and loving. Whereas, at present, we can only be present to each other and to God through transitory, limited acts of knowing and loving, if our lives are to be as open-ended as we can imagine, somehow our present acts must be brought to an unending consummation. This is the point at which Christian faith in the presence of God to us now and the possibility of bringing our presence to each other and God to a lasting consummation in eternity reflect back on what we do now, make the whole of life open-ended, and by doing so, add a depth dimension to it.

In the light of faith, death is seen as a transition to a new and fuller mode of life in the Spirit. This belief makes life genuinely open-ended and is consistent with our understanding of the role of suffering and death to self throughout life. Just as these are an integral part of the dynamic in all experiences that lead to personal growth, and so to an increase in life, so too, death, at the end of our lives is a transitory experience leading to a consummation and the fullness of life. Heaven is not understood as a place, but as a relationship with God that came into existence at the moment of Christ's resurrection. At that moment Jesus' humanity entered into a new fullness of life in the presence of his Father, which relationship is referred to as heaven. At that moment, the risen Christ, in and through his humanity, was given the power to send the Spirit to dwell in the hearts of all those who are spiritually united to him. Thus, we see that the purpose of Jesus' passion-death-resurrection is to facilitate his presence to us here on earth through the sending of his Spirit; and, at the same time, to overcome death for us, so that we too can achieve the fullness of life in the presence of God in eternity.

On the one hand, therefore, Jesus' resurrection enables him, through the indwelling Spirit, to be immanent or present to us now. On the other hand, Jesus remains transcendent. He is the beginning, sustaining foundation and end of our lives and of the whole cosmic process, which scripture tells us will be brought to fulfillment in him. As end, Jesus remains as a lure-from-beyond, as it were, a personal end toward which our lives are moving. We have absolute value and an absolute future--the fullness of life in the direct presence of God himself. Although this does not reduce the vastness of time, it personalizes it by giving it a personal end toward which it is moving.

From what we have said, we can see that there is an inherent, complementary connection between our efforts to live our lives in the presence of our neighbour and God here on earth and resurrected life in eternity. Eternity in the presence of God is not unrelated to our lives in the presence of God and others now, nor can it be reduced to merely a prize or reward promised on the condition that we perform certain acts here on earth. Such an approach does not highlight the inherent connection between the present process of living and the reward. Heaven is the culmination of the whole of life on earth, of everything we are and do, when all of these are seen in terms of our mutual, personal presence to God and

neighbour. In fact, as indicated above, the possibility of "getting to heaven" is a necessary culmination of the process of life, if what we are and what
we do now are to have any ultimate, comprehensive
meaning and value at present.

If we transpose these thoughts into the language
of means and ends, the ultimate meaning of the process
of living here and now is in the final end of this
process--in the total, personal presence of God to us
in eternity. This end is already being partially
realized by us now, through our daily experiences of
living in God's presence and through our commitment
to the presence and needs of our neighbours. In fact,
the only way we can achieve that future end is by
wholehearted commitment to the present out of which
it must be built. This does not imply that we establish the kingdom of God; that is the work of God himself. We are, however, co-creators who, through the
grace of God operative in us, build up world community
and the Body of Christ at one and the same time. We
cannot hope to achieve salvation individually apart
from our efforts to help others achieve it too or
without becoming deeply involved in the secular struggles, issues and aspirations of people here and now.
We cannot attain God's absolute future, if we do not
commit ourselves to fostering a human present and
future on earth. There can be no escape for the
Christian from commitment to earthly realities, and
no opposition established in principle between our
spiritual life and our life of service in the world.

Transposed into biblical language, what we are
discussing here is "the already" and "the not yet."
The former is the redemptive presence of God which
has already been achieved for us through Christ's
passion-death-resurrection. However, the fullness of
this presence is "not yet" experienced, nor will it
be experienced in time. It is yet to be achieved,
and will not be ours until we enter the fullness of
the kingdom in eternity. As we have already seen in
a slightly different context, the *kairos*, the present moment of salvation, is the moment to which we
must commit ourselves completely, because it is the
meeting point between the redemption achieved by
Christ and the fullness of eternal life.

In spite of the fact that an understanding of
eternal or resurrected life is so important for understanding life here and now, the notion of eternal

life remains ill-defined and psychologically unappealing for many people. Our whole approach to time
as personal presence helps to highlight the meaning
and relevance of eternity. Where time is regarded
exclusively in terms of a succession of minutes, the
very concept of eternity comes across as endless time,
regardless of theologians' most ardent efforts to
conceptualize it as entirely outside of and incapable
of being measured in terms of time. Eternal life is
not measurable in terms of time, because it is the
fullness or consummation of time. A life that would
continue in an endless succession of fragmented,
fleeting, finite encounters would achieve no genuine
consummation, and so would be unappealing. But eternal life is something quite different from that. It
is an experience of total encounter with the infinite,
incomprehensible person of God, as he is in himself.
Thus, eternal life is the end, the goal, the fullness
of time. It is the consummation of all that we experience in a limited manner in time now.

We have seen that our present experience of God's
presence is through the created participation he gives
us in his life. This presence in time now is limited
and sequential, regardless of the fact that it is not
only open to, but will be consummated in, his infinite, direct, personal presence in eternity. His
presence to us now is mediated to us through time.
The experience of being in the direct presence of
infinite personhood, however, will be neither temporal, sequential nor fragmented. It will be a direct,
personal encounter, which is neither mediated nor
fragmented into successive moments. It will not only
be outside of time as we know and experience it, but
will be the fulfillment of all we experience in time.
We shall experience, to the extent of our own individual capacities, the direct presence of God as he is
in himself through a loving knowledge that embraces
God and people. The direct, unmediated presence of
God will enable us to be directly present to others
and fully present to ourselves. That is to say,
through an ongoing act of loving knowledge of God,
who is the foundation of personhood, we shall achieve
total self-awareness. Thus, eternal life in the presence of God also consummates our present striving for
self-knowledge and personal identity, two of our most
central, spiritual aspirations. This means that all
our positive efforts now to be truly present to ourselves, to others and to God will be brought to fulfillment in eternity. This fact makes life psycholog-

ically open-ended and encourages us to commit ourselves to it wholeheartedly.

Toward the Fullness of Life in the Spirit

Having already indicated the possibility of not
only experiencing, but also growing in the presence
of God in our daily lives, we can now concentrate on
the goal of the Christian, which is to live more and
more fully in the Spirit. Ephesians 3:16-21, a prayer
and doxology, is a complex biblical teaching regarding
growth in the fullness of the Spirit. Paul prays
that the Father, through his infinite majesty, holiness and saving power, will grant inner, spiritual
growth to the Ephesians through the power of the indwelling Holy Spirit. The Holy Spirit, who is the
Spirit of the risen Christ, enables Christ to be present in the hearts of believers through faith. Thus,
having received the gift of divine love and being
firmly grounded in it, the Ephesians will be built up
in spiritual union with all others open to the working
of the Spirit. They will develop the strength to
come to see Christ's cosmic role in the rebirth of
the whole world, to grasp the infinite dimensions of
the mystery of salvation, and, above all, to experience the infinite, universal love of Christ on which
salvation depends.

The love of Christ, which is proven by his redemptive acceptance of death, is identical to the love of
the Father and is made available by the power of the
Spirit. Knowledge of this love cannot be grasped in
the same way as philosophical knowledge and far exceeds it. It is known or experienced in the contemplative or intuitive awareness of the believer who
knows s/he is loved by God. Through this love, believers will eventually be filled with the fullness
of God. Because Christ possesses the fullness of
divine life, those who receive it form his Body and
become part of the new creation that is being built.
The incarnation itself is being brought to its fulfillment in the Church as believers reach out and
grow in the love of God and its transforming power.

It is evident, therefore, that to understand fully
what it is to be human or to be personally present to
others in the fullest sense, we must go beyond a study
of people apart from God. Since the incarnation, we

cannot know what it is to be authentically human apart
from a knowledge of God, having become a human person
in Jesus of Nazareth and being present to us in and
through the indwelling Spirit of Christ. Our meaning
and fulfillment is inextricably bound up with our
end--the gift of God's presence on earth consummated
in resurrected life. Nor is it possible to know God
apart from his having united himself with us. To
attempt to understand God apart from his historical
union with us in Christ is to try to understand him
in a vacuum.

From the first moments of creation, when the
Spirit of God hovered over the primordial waters, the
Spirit generated life. Throughout the whole creative-
redemptive process, the Spirit constantly generates
the life of God in his people. In the New Covenant,
it is the Spirit who generated the life of Jesus in
Mary. Christ indicates to his disciples that unless
he is raised up he will not be able to send the Pa-
raclete, the Spirit, to dwell with and generate his
life in them. It was through his passion-death-
resurrection that Christ was given a new power in his
humanity to send the Spirit to abide in a permanent
way in the believing community. The Pentecost event
narrates this bestowal. Since Pentecost, the Spirit
consistently generates the life and love of God, first
in the believing community as a whole, and then in
individual members baptized into that community. It
is also the role of the Spirit to generate the life
of Christ in the eucharist, so that it becomes spiritual nourishment for those who receive it.

It is the presence of the Holy Spirit dwelling in
the Christian community that makes it the special
locus of God's presence to us. In this communal context, the Spirit bestows on believers the love, freedom, peace and life of God. Thus, the role of the
indwelling Spirit is central in every mode by which
God's life and love are present to us. The presence
of the Holy Spirit is the key to the presence of God
to us and to the transformation of our lives that
this entails. As John indicates, the Christian life
is made possible, not primarily through human love,
but through the love of God: "this is the love I
mean: not our love for God, but God's love for us
when he sent his Son to be the sacrifice that takes
our sins away" (1 Jn. 4:10).

Having received the gift of God's infinite love,

our responsibility is simply to use this freely given
ability to respond in kind. Our response to God
through our neighbour far exceeds the minimal requirements of a legal response, because it becomes a freely
chosen response of our whole being in love. Self-
revealing, self-communicating love becomes the meaning
of life. Once we let the Jesus event become part of
us, his Spirit is present to us in the full meaning
of presence that has been used throughout this entire
work: he contributes to the development of our internal constitution so that we are transformed interiorly. In turn, we body forth his spiritual presence
to others through what we are and do. Human encounters become encounters with God, so that in everything
we do Christ becomes "the Way, the Truth and the Life"
(Jn. 14:6). We "dwell in love;" we "abide in Christ;"
we become members of "the Body of Christ." Love, freedom and truth are not simply realities we have or
possess; they become so much a part of our constitution that we live them.

To understand how this process begins and continues in us, we must turn to Christ's death and resurrection and to our baptism. Just as Jesus overcame
sin and death through his passion-death-resurrection,
so too we are baptized into the death of Christ. In
order to understand the significance of these realities, we shall look at them as passover events. For
the Hebrew people, the passover was liberation from
slavery in Egypt to freedom to live with their God in
the promised land. It was first a flood experience
in which they were overwhelmed by the activity of God
on their behalf, but they did not learn immediately
to give themselves over to Yahweh and to rely on him.
Their subsequent desert experience was a time of pur-
gation through which they learned to stop clinging to
themselves as the source of their life, liberty and
well-being. They were disciplined and pruned to help
them to remain open to Yahweh's support, to wait on
his presence and to persevere in his life and service.

In a similar manner, Jesus' passion-death-resurrection was a passover in which he was overwhelmed by
the agony of abandonment, betrayal and impending
death. Yet he remained constant to his identity as
Son of the Father, and abandoned his entire self to
God. God remained faithful to him, resurrected him
and gave him the power to send us his Spirit. Our
baptism into the death of Christ is also a passover
event. It is much more than simply a washing away of

sin.   In baptism we allow the flood to overwhelm us.
The death we experience is death to sin, slavery and
the law; our rebirth is to life in the Spirit.   This
passover from Egypt to the promised land, for us, is
a passover from a life in this world, in which we
cling to our own powers as the source of our action,
to a life in this world in which we allow God to be
the source of all that we are and do.

The cross is not simply a symbol of death and
suffering, although these are an inherent part of
it.   It is ultimately a symbol of a passover from
slavery and all that kills to freedom and all that
gives life in the Spirit.   The slavery and death from
which we need to be delivered are the slavery and
death caused by dichotomizing ourselves into being
both activator and activated.   When we cling to ourselves as the source, we have to determine good and
evil, and the good we achieve is simply our own.
Because we have not opened ourselves to allow the
Spirit to dwell in us and move us from within, everything comes from us.   Our actions do not flow from
his insight, power and love as their source.   Although
they may be objectively good, because we are clinging
to our fallen condition (life apart from God), both
the good and evil we perform in this condition are
fallen.   They lack the redeeming power of actions
that would flow from the power of the Spirit, if we
allowed him to be God in us.   Our passover is a transition from living in the created world, as if we
were its source and the source of all we do, to living
in the created world in a way that allows God to be
God.   It is a transition from an ungodly to a godly
way of life.

We saw that the Hebrews experienced the desert as
a time during which they learned to rely on and yield
to God's activity in and through them.   So too, desert
experience is an ongoing part of the Christian life.
Life is a constant movement away from moments of temptation, where in one way or another we are moved to
turn back to slavery.   It is a constant process of
growth in which we translate into very concrete terms,
from day to day, our belief that God is sufficient
for us.

Let us recall Dewey's analysis of the second phase
of all experience.   It is a process of interaction in
which a balance between doing and suffering is required for growth.   It is possible to see here the

compatibility of the cross with the nature of human experience itself. For Dewey, suffering enters every human experience in its transitional phase, as a necessary element, if the experience is to attain a consummation and personal growth or life are to be achieved. In the Christian life, the suffering symbolized by the cross enters as an inherent element in our passover from a self-centered to a God-centered life. The transitional phase in experience and the passover phase in redemption can be one and the same thing. The hardships and sufferings we encounter daily can be instrumental in helping us achieve both self-realization and the fullness of life and freedom in the Spirit, if we let them. The same actions performed willingly by us, with the indwelling Spirit as their source, enable us to foster human community (the secular city) and the spiritual union of people sharing the life of the Spirit (the Body of Christ) at one and the same time.

In what has been said here we grasp real, theological insight into what I said earlier, namely, that in one sense nothing changes when a person begins to live in the Spirit; and yet, in another sense, everything is changed. The person who begins to open her/himself to the working of the Spirit still lives in the same world. The same problems remain, and they need solutions requiring human knowledge, technological expertize and time. Yet there is a radical change in that person to the extent that s/he is attuned to the inner, divine wisdom, love and freedom that are capable of transforming her/his human powers and extending them beyond their finite limitations. Grace builds on nature, not in the sense of simply adding a supernatural layer to it, like a second story in a home. Grace operates more like a leaven that permeates the dough of nature, transforming it from within and adding a depth dimension that enables us to transcend our own, natural capacity to perform free, loving action.

There is a genuine depth dimension added to human freedom by grace that liberates us from sin, slavery and the law, so that we are free to live by the life of the Spirit within us. Paul expresses this notion to the Galatians when he says, "through the Law I am dead to the Law, so that now I can live for God. I have been crucified with Christ, and I live now not with my own life but with the life of Christ who lives in me" (Gal. 2:19-20). He expresses the transformation that has occurred within himself and us even more starkly when he states that "Life to me, of course, is Christ" (Phil. 1:21).

It is also in the context of the indwelling Holy Spirit that we can realize our greatest possibilities to be truthful and honest. It is the confidence and trust that accompany love that make it possible for us to accept the truth about ourselves and to honestly face our own limitations, sufferings and sinfulness. We open ourselves to truth and become more and more honest almost in direct proportion to our experience of being loved. God is absolute truth and love; in him truth and love are one and the same. The indwelling Spirit brings us into direct encounter with God's truth and love for us. The more we grow in the life of the Spirit in us, the closer is our union with God's absolute truth and love.

Truth, like faith, belongs to the realm of experience or doing. It must be lived. Thus, we cannot grow in the life of the Spirit if we do not use the gift of the Spirit to love and serve our neighbours. In this, as in everything else, God does not force us. He takes the initiative and evokes a response from us. The indwelling Spirit generates the life of the Son in us, and in so doing calls us to open ourselves and to respond to each other as adopted sons of God. Our direct encounter with God present in us unites us as sisters and brothers, because we are united to him. Those who share the life of God, share each other's lives. Through our union with the absolute truth of God, we attain love, truthfulness and honesty, both in ourselves and in our interactions with others. We learn to cling to the truth in love and to speak it out of love. In this context truth unites rather than divides. As Augustine states so clearly, people love the truth when it enlightens, but hate it when it reproaches them. Fellowship in the Son radically exceeds the warmth and friendliness of human associations and clubs, and enables us to attain depths of truth and honesty otherwise unattainable, because the presence of God is the unifying principle that binds us to each other.

From what we have just said, it is evident that the movement toward the fullness of life in the Spirit is a lifelong process. The aim for the individual is to become another Christ, that is, to assimilate his life to the point where we think and respond in every situation as Jesus would if he were the responder. From the communal perspective, the aim is to build up the Body of Christ; and in so doing, co-operate with the work of God in establishing the kingdom on earth. In all of this, we attempt to focus more and more clearly on the will of God for us. This is a formidable task made possible by using Jesus as our model. Christ maintained his identity as Son of the Father, not only by serving people, but by taking time to pray. He listened to the Father and spoke what the Father gave him to say. By hearing, which is the biblical meaning for obeying, he came to know and obey the will of God for him, even when it was most difficult. The providence of God for Jesus was the same as it is for us; it is his ongoing divine presence.

It is not possible here to discuss all the ways by which we grow in the life of the Spirit. I shall bring my discussion to a close by commenting on three modes of divine presence selected for more pastoral than theological reasons. The first is regular attendance at eucharistic liturgy or other forms of weekly service. It is the faith of numerous Christian denominations that the celebration of the eucharist is the central act of worship of the Christian life and that toward which all other forms of worship and service are oriented. Yet, in spite of the fact that in eucharistic celebration God is present to the assembled community in the reading of the scripture, the words of the homilist, and, most directly, in the body and blood, numerous Christians absent themselves on the grounds that they "get very little out of it." Let me point out, from the perspective of personal presence, one reason why this is happening.

A personal relationship with God is similar to any other personal relationship; one has to work at it and maintain it on a regular basis. If a young man, for no serious reason, does not talk to and spend time with his girl on a fairly regular basis, it comes as no great surprise to anyone that after a few months she is no longer his girl. Yet, it is much harder for people to realize that if they do not take time out to communicate with God in private prayer and in common worship on a regular basis, after a while God is no longer their God. They have unconsciously and indeliberately fallen into the habit of living their lives on their own. God is excluded from their decision-making and ordinary pursuits. When they take time to attend a eucharistic liturgy, they approach it almost as an outsider who needs to be re-initiated into the spirit and life of the assembled community before being able to experience the presence of the Lord in a meaningful way.

It takes time to open our hearts and minds to God, just as it takes time to open ourselves to other people. Too frequently, by the time we have begun to be open to the point where a genuine, satisfying encounter with God in liturgy is possible, the service is over. This is especially true if we have behaved in a way that has disrupted our relationship with God. In such a situation, little satisfaction is experienced in God's presence until some form of reconciliation has occurred. This takes time. Thus, without in any way reducing the responsibility of clergy to upgrade the quality of the liturgies they celebrate, all Christians have to take responsibility for preparing themselves personally to receive the gift of God's presence available to them in eucharistic celebration.

In discussing the ways people in our society today experience the presence of God concretely in their lives, one ought not to overlook the numerous, anonymous, twelve step programs that are springing up among those who find themselves addicted to some form of compulsive behaviour. Those involved voluntarily form groups to help themselves overcome alcohol or drug addiction, over-eating, gambling or destructive, compulsive emotional or sexual behaviour. These people cut across denominational lines. They come together to support each other in their common affliction. These twelve step programs are spiritual programs. Those who seek help begin by admitting that they are powerless over their addiction and that their lives have become unmanageable. They come to believe that there is a Power greater than themselves who can restore them to sanity; and they make a decision to turn their lives and wills over to the care of God, as they understand him personally. They make a moral inventory of their lives that is fearless; and admit to themselves and God in a rigorously truthful and honest way the nature of their wrongs. They open themselves to God, as they understand him; and ask him to remove their character defects and shortcomings. Through prayer and meditation, they seek to improve their conscious contact with God, praying for knowledge of his will and the strength to fulfill

it. As they work their program in their private
lives, they try to bring their message to others in
need. They also meet on a regular basis for sharing
and mutual support.[12]

It is not at all uncommon for members of these
programs to state clearly that they experience the
presence of God in their midst at their meetings.
Although they cannot explain it, they also acknowledge
that their Higher Power is in some way present to
them liberating them from their addiction and restor-
ing sanity to their lives. Where people turn over
their lives to God, as they understand him, in such a
complete way, surely the promise in Matthew's gospel
is being fulfilled: "if two of you on earth agree to
ask anything at all, it will be granted to you by my
Father in heaven. For where two or three meet in my
name, I shall be there with them" (Mt. 18:19-20).

While acknowledging that these programs do not
promote any specific religion's understanding of God,
it is legitimate, in the light of Christian spiritu-
ality, to recognize the working of the Spirit in these
meetings. The Spirit is saving these people from
their destructive behaviour and their sins (to the
extent that their compulsive, addicted behaviour might
be sinful), and is healing and divinizing them in
their area of weakness and need. It is also worth
noting that the participants experience the active
presence of their Higher Power in their lives, to the
extent that they are rigorously honest and truthful
in turning their lives over to him and being faithful
to their program. For some, the spiritual power of
God experienced through the fellowship, sharing and
support of their fellow members, is their first, real
experience of church. In my estimation, the deeply
religious and spiritual nature of these movements
ought to be more readily acknowledged. I see only
one serious risk. Because of the intensity and effectiveness of this mode of experiencing the presence
of God in their lives, some members might erroneously
conclude that this is the only essential mode of encountering God for them. This, it seems to me, is a
dangerous reductionism.

The final mode of divine presence I shall discuss
is contemplative prayer. I choose it, rather than
other methods of prayer such as recitation of formal
prayers, prayer of petition, meditation and charis-
matic prayer, for a number of reasons. Although con-

templative knowledge provides us with a loving, holistic knowledge, our society is not at ease with it as it is with empirical reasoning. It is a relatively simple form of prayer within the capacity of all, in spite of the fact that it is commonly thought to be the activity of a spiritual elite. Finally, it is the most direct and intimate prayer of presence.

Contemplative prayer does not require complicated methods or the mastery of special techniques. It is not another action a person has to perform in the sense of another activity that will simply keep one busy with God, instead of being busy with people. As in all redemptive activity, God takes the initiative; we must depend totally on him and the gift of his grace. Contemplative prayer presupposes a willingness to open ourselves to God in simple faith, hope and love, and then a readiness to watch and wait for his presence. This simple, but radical, openness to God is not only an attentive, waiting desire; it is a willingness to be empty before him. We must empty our hearts and minds of all our accomplishments and problems, so that we stand before God without righteousness and without anything to show, prove or argue, if we are to succeed at praying the prayer of presence. In appearing before God like the publican in our emptiness and uselessness, rather than filled with our own usefulness and strength like the pharisee, we acknowledge God's priority over us.[13] This is a way of calling out, "Come, Lord Jesus; feed us; fill us with your Spirit."

In contemplative prayer we have a final instance of what we have seen throughout this entire work, namely, that being honest and truthful are not only intimately connected, but directly proportional to achieving personal presence in its fullest sense. Acknowledging our emptiness and uselessness in relation to God is neither a demeaning act nor one of false humility. It is a true expression of our radical dependence on God. We are a gift of God to ourselves and to each other. What we accomplish, we accomplish by the help of his grace.

Prayer of presence is more intimate than conversation or dialogue with God. It more accurately expresses falling in love with God. It manifests an extremely intimate relationship in which the person praying comes to know God more by love than by reason. Thus, words become less important as silent communion

increases.[14]   In fact, it is neither inaccurate nor
disrespectful to refer to the contemplative prayer of
presence as intercourse with God.   This phrase comes
close to expressing our openness, receptivity and
honest dependence on God as well as the depth of
giving and true commitment to him that are involved
in contemplation.   The person who pursues this depth
of presence and union with God is called to open her/
himself to Christ in his passion-death-resurrection
and to be led through the dryness and darkness of
preparation and waiting to deeper moments of
intimacy.[15]

     As the prayer of presence awakens us to find God
in our own hearts, it also enables us to see him in
the people and situations around us.   God present in
us recognizes God present in the world about us.
Contemplation, therefore, opens us to a whole new way
of seeing reality and of appreciating the breadth and
depth of the incarnation.   A brief period of time set
aside daily for this type of prayer enables us to
become increasingly receptive to the working of the
Spirit, and growth in the Spirit brings us closer to
each other.   Instead of experiencing abandonment and
alienation, those who practise contemplation, experience a sense of direction.   When God is seen at the
core of reality, connections previously unnoticed
appear, and life becomes more integrated and meaningful.   The experience of God's inner presence becomes
a stable source of motivation and commitment that
energizes us to meet our commitments with zeal and
satisfaction.[16] Without doubt, contemplative prayer
and eucharistic liturgy are our most efficacious,
religious means of growing in the Spirit and developing community.

     Throughout this work we have moved from under-
standing fundamentals regarding personal presence,
honesty and truthfulness, through an exposition of
various modes of personal presence and obstacles to
achieving them at present, to suggestions for creating
a future in the presence of God.   We saw that understanding personal presence challenges us to delve
more deeply into the mystery of what it is to be
human.   This search ultimately opened our inquiry
into our participation in the life of God, because the
human and divine are inseparable since the incarnation.   We saw that our most satisfying achievements
are acts of knowing, loving and enjoying each other.
Our attempt to assure genuine open-endedness and

meaning for these activities also opened us to the fittingness of eternal life in the presence of God.

Finally, we saw that we are challenged like never before to develop a world community. In fact, in spite of what appear to be overwhelming, personal obstacles in the way of this movement, all the tech- nical forces in society continue to increase the con- nections that are forcing mankind to become one close- ly knit community. Overcoming the personal obstacles to developing world community is the most urgent moral, spiritual and religious challenge we face to- day. This examination of personal presence highlights the truth that human presence and love tend to focus on individual people, whereas God's presence and love are for all. This study challenges us to honestly face the fact that we are called today, with even greater urgency than in the past, to open ourselves to the presence of God, because his presence will enable us to extend our presence to all people. With the aid of God's indwelling Spirit we shall succeed in developing the personalistic future we are called to create.

Notes

1. Pieper, pp. 40, 42-43.
2. Ibid., pp. 17, 56-58.
3. Adrian van Kaam and Susan Muto, *Practicing the Prayer of Presence*, (Denville, N.J.: Dimension Books, 1980), pp. 16-20.
4. Nouwen, pp. 27-32.
5. Sebastian Moore, *The Inner Loneliness* (New York: Crossroads, 1982), pp. 2, 57-58, 60.
6. Ibid., pp. 1, 22-23, 25, 33-34.
7. Ibid., pp. 58-59. Those who refer to Moore will note that throughout I have avoided his termi- nology regarding God "halving" the human whole. I judge his insights to be valid and very helpful. We agree that the relational nature of people leads them to experience a certain incompleteness because they need to participate in each other's lives in order to be and to know themselves. We also agree that this incompleteness is experienced by people in their sexual identity and their need to communicate and participate in the life of another through sexual union. Nevertheless, in spite of this incompleteness, I maintain that individual people are wholes who re-

late with each other as wholes and are enriched through this mutual participation. To express female or male identity in terms of knowing oneself as "only half of the human whole" or creation in terms of God's "'halving' of the human whole" is at least inadequate terminology, as I see it. This approach creates a number of consequences I am unwilling to accept.

8.   Ibid., pp. 67-68.
9.   Ibid., pp. 2, 24, 67.
10.   Ibid., pp. 14-15.
11.   Nouwen, p. 99
12.   *Twelve Steps and Twelve Traditions* (New York: Alcoholics Anonymous World Services, Inc., 1953), pp. 5-9. What has been presented here is simply selected elements of the twelve steps of Alcoholics Anonymous. In general, these are adopted by the other anonymous groups.
13.   van Kaam and Muto, pp. 52-53, 57, 64, 66-67.
14.   Ibid., pp. 58, 94-96.
15.   Ibid., pp. 66, 90-92.
16.   Ibid., pp. 61-62, 69, 102-04.